Nuggets of Writing Gold

by Leeann Betts and Donna Schlachter

ISBN10: 1943688052
ISBN13: 978-1-943688-05-0

Published by PLS Bookworks, Denver, Colorado

Where Publishing Dreams Become Reality

Check our website for upcoming releases:

www.PLSBookwords.com

FOREWORD

This book was written as a helps for writers, a one-stop-shopping place to find the answers and resources you need to keep you pounding away at the keyboard day after day when everything inside you screams: QUIT!

It is by no means an exhaustive dissertation on the subject of writing. It is not filled with rules. It is not the Ten Commandments of writing.

Rather, we hope you will pick and choose what you need. And we expect that eventually you will read the entire book, because at some point along the way, you're going to need some encouragement, some direction, some teaching on craft, some insight into how to use that little bit of research that just won't leave you alone. Or you're going to be registered for a conference you've never attended before, and you'll be scared out of your wits. Or you will want to go to a conference, but don't know where to start looking for the one for you.

If you get any benefit out of this book, it isn't because we are so witty or such great teachers--it will be because you applied what you read here.

Blessings for the road, and let's keep in touch.

Leeann Betts and Donna Schlachter

Donna@LiveByTheWord.com

Other Books
Written as Leeann Betts & Donna Schlachter:

By the Numbers **series featuring Carly Turnquist, forensic accountant**

No Accounting for Murder
There Was a Crooked Man
Unbalanced
Five and Twenty Blackbirds
Broke, Busted, and Disgusted
Hidden Assets
Petty Cash
A Deadly Dissolution
Silent Partner
In the Money
Missing Deposits
Risk Management

Mysterious Ink Bookstore **series featuring Margie Hanson, librarian**

The Game is Afoot
Little Grey Cells
Heavier Than Broken Hearts
Nothing is Easy – coauthored with Donna Schlachter

The Worst-Kept Secret in "Always a Wedding Planner Romance Collection"

Counting the Days: a 31-day devotional
In Search of Christmas Past – a novel

Nuggets of Writing Gold -- articles and essays on writing.
More Nuggets of Writing Gold – more articles and essays on writing

Written as Donna Schlachter:

***Mended by God* series – bringing healing and wholeness to your heart and soul**

Broken Dreams, Mended Heart
Broken Dreams, Mended Family
Broken Dreams, Mended Marriage

I Do – Again: a devotional for remarrieds
Second Chances and Second Cups: A short story collection.
The Physics of Love
The Mystery of Christmas Inn, Colorado
Christmas Under the Stars
Transformation – a devotional
Time Will Tell – Christmas Under Main Street series
From Here to There
A Midwife's Tale (Amazon Vella publication)
Zero Guilt Calories – Sweet Sprinkles: The Limited Edition

***The Oregon Trail Mysteries* series**

Kate
A Pink Lady Thanksgiving

Healing the Wounded Heart series

Testing Tessa
Justice for Julia

Written in Love series

Cactus Lil and the City Slicker
Cactus Lil's Big City Debut

Hearts of the Pony Express series

Hollenberg Hearts
Hollow Hearts
Hearts of Julesburg

Mail-Order Brides series

The New Hope Train
Road to Freedom

Mail Order Papa series

A King for Kinsella

Prairie Roses series

Calli

Kate

Tina

Reclusive Man series

Dianna's Dilemma

Hers to Redeem series

David's Difficulty

A Christmas Ridge Romance

A Mommy by Christmas

Merry Little Mysteries Anthology

A Mistletoe Mystery

The Recipe Box Series

Recipe for Disaster, 1784 Book 1

Cooking Up Trouble, 1834 Book 2

Switchboard Sisterhood Series

Juliette

Morgana

The Suffrage Spinster series

Rollie's Riddle

Theresa's Talent

Courting Chaos series

Kaihtlyn's Choice

Available at Online Retailers and Fine Booksellers:

Quiet Moments Alone with God: a devotional

100 Answers to 100 Questions About Loving Your Husband

Detours of the Heart – MISSadventure Brides Romance Collection

Coming Soon Titles

I've got many projects in the works, with books planned for 2024 and beyond. Many are tentative release dates.

Historical

Recipe Box series #3 May 2024
Matchmaker's Mixup series June 2024
Hearts of the Pony Express #4 August 2024
A Sleigh Ride for Ruby November 2024
Recipe Box #4 December 2024
Hot Air Balloon story February 2025
Mail-Order Romance series May 2025
Recipe Box series #5 September 2025
National Parks Bride: Cecelia October 2025
Recipe Box series #6 January 2026
A Legacy in Love 2-in-1 April 2026

Other Historical Projects (tentative titles)

The Hello Girls
Mountain Mining Mysteries
Saved By The Bell

Contemporary

Aspen Creek Historical Society
Seasoned Love
Western Heroes series

THE PASSION TO WRITE

What's Your Story?

At a recent conference, I attended a continuing education class by a firecracker of a teacher, both in her teaching style and in her personality. Rabbit trails she runs, but somehow manages to get her point across. In these classes, she actually had someone in the class keep track of her points so they could steer her back on course after she ran a tangent. Too funny!

At one point in this track, which was titled "Writing that Sings", the teacher asked us to think about what we write. Not our genre or time period, not the tag line for our website or the elevator pitch for our book, but overall, what do we write.

So here's the question for you: what do you write? For example, Kim Vogel Sawyer writes about broken people finding healing in the arms of a loving God. Sure, her tag line is gentle stories of hope, but if you look at her characters and plots, all of her characters are broken.

As I considered each of my books, I came to the realization that all of my characters are experiencing second chances -- through remarriage, through reconciliation, through overcoming their past mistakes, through overcoming their circumstances. Doesn't matter which book I consider or even which short story I look at.

So I came up with this: I write stories about second chances from a God who is bigger than our past.

I challenge you this week to think about each story you have written, are writing, or are thinking about writing, and ask: what one sentence describes what I write?

Why is this important? I'm not trying to button-hole you into a particular kind of story, but I believe, as the instructor said, when you understand what you write, you'll see your own personal walk and relationship with the Lord.

My stories of second chances from a God who is bigger than my past is right on. God has given me second chances and second-second changes many times.

While our stories aren't supposed to be autobiographical, they do convey our Christian worldview. The Lord has brought each one of us through a unique set of circumstances and equipped us with a unique set of gifts and callings, and that unique combination gives us the story of our life, carefully woven into a story others can receive, a story that points them to a loving God who can take the reader's broken story and weave it into a beautiful tapestry.

Takeaway: We each have a unique story to tell. The hard work is finding what makes the story different.

Exercises:

1. Look at the stories you write, and come up with a sentence that describes the kinds of books you write. Write it down.
2. Think about the last ten books you read that you loved. How would you describe them? Write that down.
3. Is there some overlap?

A Passion for THIS Story

In a recent conversation with my agent, Terrie Wolf, she mentioned she talks to editors occasionally who are looking for a specific book to fit a particular publishing slot. My response? "If you get any requests, let me know. Maybe I can write that book."

As I thought about this later, I wondered if I'd spoken hastily or foolishly. After all, what if they wanted a (gulp) bonnet story? Or a (double gulp) category romance? Did I really think I could write such a book? I came up with lots of reasons why I couldn't – not my genre, not my area of specialty or knowledge, never wrote one before.

And then I was reminded of the wise words spoken to me at one time, not in this context, but which I will paraphrase: Don't look for a reason not to write the story; look for a reason to write the story.

So I put on my thinking cap again. Why would I want to write a bonnet story or a category romance or a western or a sci-fi or any of the other genres I don't write? And the answer I came up with was: passion. And I'm not talking about relationship-type passion.

The kind of passion I'm talking about is the essence that starts a writer's creative juices flowing, forcing us to work past the first What if? And deeper into the next, Then What? And the next.

I would need a passion for the setting, for the characters, or for the story.

That passion would ignite the story ideas, flesh out the characters, and help me choose (or create) a believable setting. That passion would keep me writing when the words seemed blah, would keep me plotting when I didn't think anybody would want to read this story, would keep me enthused enough to press on until I typed, "The End".

Passion has nothing to do with the book as a whole, but everything to do with the components of the story. Passion is also called our Muse, that je ne sais quoi that propels us to our computer and causes our fingers to fly over the keys, the words appearing on the screen as if by osmosis.

Passion also helps us take a teensy idea and expand the details into a full-length novel. Let's take an example. Cinderella is a short story fairy tale, yet in the hands of another, become the basis for over 30 movies (based on an article on Wikipedia). No doubt each one of these movies contained details that were not included in the original story.

If we take the Cinderella story, let's go through some What If? Questions to come out to a completely different story: What if Cinderella lived with her father and siblings instead of her step-mother and step-sisters, but they were jealous of her? We'd have a story like Joseph and his coat of many colors. What if Cinderella was an orphan? We'd have a story like Oliver Twist. What if Cinderella was raised in a happy family but went her own way and left home? Prodigal son story.

So let's take the example of the (gulp) bonnet story. First I need to remember what my passion is: writing stories that show a God who is bigger than our past. My story might be about a woman journalist who decided to do a story on the Amish, falls in love with an Amish man, and marries him. "Accidentally Amish". In another story, maybe my character flees to Lancaster County, Pennsylvania, because she's on the run from the mob. "Sister Act".

Your passion for the story, characters, and setting will be different than mine, because your writing passion, that thing inside you that keeps you writing, is different. Take a few minutes and look at the theme of the stories you write and the stories you want to write. What is the common thread running through these stories? Summarize that theme, or passion, in a single sentence and leave it in the comments section. Your passion is NOT: My story is about a girl who runs away from home and gets involved in drugs and then gets saved. Your passion might be: I write stories about prodigals and their families.

Now, back to the plotting board. Let's see. A (double gulp) category romance. My female lead is a bounty hunter sent to bring back a bail jumper. My male lead is the bail jumper, an angry man, who recognizes my bounty hunter as the woman seen driving away from the scene of a bank robbery that led to a fatal car crash twenty years before where his wife was killed. Nobody was ever prosecuted for this terrible accident or for the robbery. Will she be able to convince him she isn't the person she was back then? Will he be able to see the grace and mercy of God in his own life and extend forgiveness to the woman he blames for ruining his life?

Hmmm. Might be able to make that work......

Takeaway:

If you don't have a burning passion to write a particular story, the idea will likely fizzle out like a candle in the rain.

Exercises:

1. List the top five topics/genres you like to read.
2. Look at your most recent work in progress -- does it fit with what you like to read?
3. Dig out an old project that fizzled. Did it fit with what you like to read?

What's Your Dream?

Our church was working through a series of sermons on Vision, including God's vision for our lives, and our understanding of that vision. One of the sermons encouraged each of us to write down what we believe God's vision for us, individually, is.

That was a real struggle for me. I mean, I don't have any problem with writing it down. My issue was I didn't dare write down what I hoped was God's vision for me. I really felt more comfortable putting down on paper where I am, right now. After all, that would be easy. It would mean I didn't have to strive for more. I wouldn't have to change. I could live out my vision of God's vision for me.

That's when I took a deep breath, realizing I am not where I want to be in any area of my life. Not in my marriage, my relationship with my kids and grandkids, my relationship with God, and particularly not my writing.

I realized I didn't want to just settle.

So I prayed and asked God for His vision for me.

And then I wrote down what I believe He showed me. I followed that up with a Mission Statement, and then with a paragraph I called "Manifestation" – how I will know I have achieved this vision. Check out my web site to see my version (www.LiveByTheWord.com). Feel free to use it as a guide for your own.

Scripture tells us "without a vision the people perish." (Proverbs 29:19) But we are also told to "write the vision plainly .... so others can see ... the vision has an appointed time..." (Habakkuk 2:2-3). So knowing God's plan for our lives is very important.

I encourage you to ask the Lord what He has planned for you. Ask Him what His vision for your life is. You will probably not get a timetable or a hint of when this might come to pass. But God promises us in Habakkuk it may seem slow but it will not be late (verse 3).

Then, write down what He tells you. Make a list of steps to accomplish this vision – your mission. Your ministry. Your calling and anointing. Next, make a short paragraph that combines the vision and the mission into a concise sentence or two.

Post this vision somewhere prominent. Carry it in your wallet. Keep it near your computer, so that every time you get a rejection letter or a manuscript returned, you can see it. God's vision for your life is not determined by the number of rejections, the bad reviews, the overworked-and-underpaid contracts.

God's vision for your life is determined by His complete plan, perfect and good. You've got His word on that – Jeremiah 29:11 "I know the plans I have for you," declares the LORD, "plans to prosper you and not to harm you, plans to give you hope and a future."

Takeaway: God already had a plan for your life before you were even born. He doesn't waste a single experience.

Exercises:

1. Spend some time in prayer this week seeking the Lord's will for you. Ask Him to show you two or three verses that will speak directly to your heart.
2. Look at your last projects. Do they line up with what you heard this week?
3. If not, what can you do to accomplish His will in your life?

Writing Challenge

About two years ago I completed a 14-day writing challenge where I committed to do something every day related to writing. While I thought the process would be a breeze, it was anything but. On Day 1 I was supposed to list ten books I'd like to write. This is what I put down for myself and for my alter ego who writes contemporary suspense:

Titles of 10 books I'd like to write:
Then Sings My Soul
Christmas Inn, Colorado
Klondike Gold
Honor Denied – Book 2 of the Heart of Honor Series
Denied Liability – Book 3 of the Heart of Honor Series
Collusion – Book 2 of the Florida Detective Series
Resolve – Book 3 of the Florida Detective Series
My Surrendered Heart – Book 1 of the Echo Canyon series
The Long Trail Back – Book 2 of the Echo Canyon series
Home is where the Heart is – Book 3 of the Echo Canyon series

10 Titles Leeann wants to write:
There Was a Crooked Man -- Book 2 of the By the Numbers Mystery series
Unbalanced – Book 3 of the By the Numbers Mystery series
Five and Twenty Blackbirds – Book 4 of the By the Numbers Mystery series
The Labyrinth – Book 2 in the Lighthouse Foundation series
The Landfall – Book 3 in the Lighthouse Foundation series
One Moment in Time
Of Horses and Wishes
Walking on Sunshine
Characters and Creeps
Remembering Mama

The good news is that I have written some of those books. I finished Christmas Inn, Colorado as well as My Surrendered Heart, and

Leeann has written There Was a Crooked Man and Unbalanced. She also finished One Moment in Time. Some of the others are still in progress or in the planning stages, and honestly, there are a few that I wished I'd made notes about because I don't have a clue what I was thinking at the time.

All of this goes to my point: writing a book rarely happens in a vacuum. We get an idea, a nugget of dialog, perhaps a snippet of setting, maybe even a title, and before we know it, a plot and a character or two begin to fall into place. When this happens, the creative juices begin to flow, and we are off to the races.

Unfortunately, the muse can flee as quickly as she appeared, so that what once seemed like such a great idea fizzles like wet firecrackers.

What do we do when that happens? We can press on, force the story, force the ending, and maybe end up with something worth revising.

We can start at the beginning, with the gem that got us excited about this story, and see if we can find the true essence of the story in a different direction.

We can toss out the whole thing and start all over with a new project.

Or we can do a little of each, and treat it like a tossed salad of words.

In my case, for example, Remembering Mama was probably an idea for a coming of age story about a girl whose mother died when she was young and the impact that had on her life. I've seen several books about that topic in recent years. So maybe I need to switch the story around a little bit. Maybe Mama didn't die, but ran away from her abusive husband, leaving her children behind. And the father forbade the children to ever mention their mother. But they do. The more he says forget her, the more they get together in secret to remember her. Except they don't have much to go on because they were young, and so they make up a lot of the details. Until one day the father dies, and the mother comes back. And she isn't anything like what they remember. Bittersweet for the mother and the children.

Don't be afraid to abandon one story idea in favor of another. All writing is good exercise for the brain, so nothing is wasted.

Takeaway: Writing requires discipline, but don't try to shove a square peg story into a round hole outline.

Exercises:

1. Make a list of ten books you'd like to write. Make some notes, maybe a couple of sentences, about the story so you'll remember it later.
2. Choose the title that excites you the most. This would be the one where you can already see the main character and what's going to happen to her.
3. Start writing that story.

14-Day Writing Challenge

Following are some ideas from the same 14-day writing challenge I mentioned in the previous article. I will include my responses to get you started.

Day 2 – create a character with personality traits of someone you love but with physical characteristics of someone you don't care for.

From Donna:

Grace is exactly like her name--full of love and compassion for the underdog, always looking for the silver lining in every cloud. She likes to extend a helping hand to people, and would do it more often, except she's crippled by arthritis from her neck down to the tips of her toes.

From Leeann:

Charles is patient and kind, a man who attracts women and repels men because of his don't-argue-with-me-you-won't-win attitude, a man who loves Jesus with all his heart. His only problem is his teeth. He doesn't have many, and the ones he does have are black and broken, so he doesn't smile much.

Day 3 -- Write a setting based on the most beautiful place you've ever seen.

From Donna:
The wagon ruts ahead seemed to dwarf even the huge Conestoga wagons. The walls of rock-hard soil that rimmed the trail were so tall Emma couldn't see over them. She looked behind her at the emigrants struggling up the rocky path, urging their mules and oxen and horses forward. One mare a couple of wagons back slipped and fell heavily, pulling its teammate to the ground as well. The driver cursed and got down, stepping carefully from the brake to the wheel hub to the dirt. There was no jumping from the five-foot height of the wagon. A body could snap a leg or stumble and hit their head. Maybe even die. Emma looked ahead. As far as she could see, the trail had been dug deep into the soil. After six days of this, she felt like she was walking through a perpetual grave. And yet she'd never seen anything so beautiful in all her life. Knowing that thousands of emigrants had already traveled this trail to freedom, and thousands more followed in her wake, gave her the strength and courage to carry on. She was part of something bigger than herself.

From Leeann:
Down below, the water sparkled in the sun like a million jewels floated just below the surface. Carolyn looked as far out to sea as she could. A cruise ship entered the harbor, seeking refuge from the coming storm. As the vessel neared, passengers lined the decks, waving to the people on the beach below. Carolyn wondered about these people. Where did they live? What kind of jobs did they do? She looked to her left and marveled at the swimmers so far out from shore, at the dive boats coming in at the end of the day, at the sunbathers clustered around the pool. The white sand looked so inviting. She wiggled her bare toes, remembering the silky feel on her feet. Poolside, a waiter moved with grace and balance amongst the guests, removing empty glasses and replacing them with new drinks. Sweat dribbled down the sides of the

beer bottles like a rain shower, and people laughed as if they didn't have a care in the world.

Day 4--Write a letter to an agent telling her how wonderful you are.

From Donna:

Dear Agent:

I am enclosing my entire manuscript because I know you're going to love it and ask to see the entire thing anyway so here it is. Tomorrow I will mail the next seven books in the series. Once you've read them, I'd appreciate if you could send them back, since I paid to have them typed from my handwritten notes, and this is the only copy I have. So don't lose it.

I've had several agents who said I wasn't ready to be published, but I figure, if my mother likes my writing, what do they know? So, I trust you'll appreciate my work and be ready to sign me and get me a six-figure advance.

From Leeann:

Dear Agent:

If you only knew how lucky you were that I am contacting you, you would count your lucky stars twice. Since you don't know, I'll tell you.

I have already sent my work to over 300 agents before you, and received replies from about 50. I trust you are not so rude to ignore my letter.

I am willing to write a book every three years and send it to you so you can edit and revise to your heart's content, and then get it published, because every book I write will be a number one bestseller. My critique group says so, and I believe them.

In exchange, you can list my name on your website so you can draw other writers, but I don't want to give any commission since you'll make so much money on referrals you won't need my money.

If you can fly here from New York next week, we can meet on Wednesday at eleven. For a half hour. I've got a busy day planned.

Day 5--Write a 20-line poem about a memorable event in your life

From Donna:

When I was only five,
And such a cute child was I
A boy from down the street
Stole my bike.
I walked right down and hit him
And pushed him to the ground.
I rode my bike back home
And told my dad.
My dad thought that was good
And told me so.
But the boy's dad
He got mad
And banged upon our door.
But when he learned
What his son had done
He wasn't mad at me anymore.
So now if you take what's mine
Be prepared to stand and fight.
I might not be big and strong
But I am awful bright.

From Leeann:

I hate to look the fool.
I recall that day in school
When the basset hound came into our classroom.
He wandered among the desks
And made some boys laugh.
And some of the girls cried
But not me.
I picked that dog right up
And balanced him on my hip
And walked him down to the door out to the street.

I sent him on his way
And went back to my class
Where all the kids laughed at me.
You see, when I picked up the dog
His hind leg hooked in my skirt.
I didn't feel the draught
I didn't know a thing.
And so I marched down the hall
Showing my bloomers.
I hate to look the fool.

Day 6-- Select a book on your shelf and pick two chapters at random. Take the first line of one chapter and the last line of the other chapter and write a short story (no more than 1000 words) using those as bookends to your story.

From Donna:

When Hope Blossoms by Kim Vogel Sawyer, Ch 12 and Ch 30

Amy inwardly groaned. When would this stupid cow ever learn that she was the boss? She picked herself up off the stall floor, righted the milking stool, and resumed her position. Nudging the cow's side with her forehead, she squeezed on the teats. "Come on, Sadie. Give."

The cow flicked her tale and turned a baleful gaze on the other occupant of the stall before turning back to chewing her cud.

Amy rubbed her hands together. Maybe Sadie didn't like cold hands. She knew she didn't. Still nothing. She stood. "Fine. I've got other things to do than stand around here coddling you. You'll give when your good and ready."

She removed the stool and the pail and went to next stall, where Midnight filled the pail in less than eight minutes. She could do this. She could prove to the banker that she had all the skills needed to run this place. She wouldn't lose her family's land. She couldn't.

Three hours later, and Amy lugged the final bucket into the milking room. While Sadie had proven reluctant, the pressure on her udder had won over her desire to be cantankerous, and Amy had been able to get nearly three gallons from her.

She poured the milk into the silver canister then used the wheelbarrow to take the container to the end of the driveway where the milk company would pick up today's milking. Seven containers. Thirty-five gallons. A whole dollar. She did a quick calculation in her head. At this rate, she'd need every cow to double its output to pay the mortgage payment on the first of the month. Fourteen days left. And that meant she couldn't spend a single penny.

The larder was nearly empty, the smokehouse was barren, and her stomach was rumbling. She needed a miracle.

As she walked back toward the house, a flash of movement caught her eye, and she paused and stared. The waist-high corn stalks in the field shivered as something worked its way through. Her knees shook at the possibilities. Wolves. Wild dogs. One of her cows. If that Sadie had broken through the fence again...

No, this was bigger than Sadie. Heavier. Noisier, too. Snorting and pawing the ground. A wild boar? That sure would be an answer to prayer and would supply meat and a good piece of hide. How was she going to deal with a wild boar? She had nothing with her except this beat-up old barrow, which was neither a weapon nor a sufficient barrier for her safety. She left the wheelbarrow and trotted back to the house, to the gun her father had kept over the fireplace. She checked the breech to make sure, but knew that the rifle was loaded. Her father saw no point in a weapon without ammunition.

The shiny wooden stock felt warm compared to the cold metal barrel, and she hefted the weapon in both hands as she scooted back the driveway. She scanned the field as she went. The tops of the corn stalks waved as if a wind was blowing through, but the day was calm and the trees were still. Except where this creature moved.

Amy jogged alongside the fence until she was broadside to the creature. Or perhaps a person? She didn't want to harm anybody. "Whoever is there, come on out. I've got a gun."

Movement paused but only for a moment. More snorts and grunts. Heavy steps coming toward her.

Then a massive head poked through the final row of cornstalks, and pink-red eyes stared at her. Dirty white hair clustered in tufts on the muzzle and around the ears, and the pink nose and lips slobbered spit that dripped to the ground in disgusting rivulets.

A white buffalo. The hide alone would pay the mortgage off. And the meat would keep her in food for six months.

The creature took several steps toward her, then bent its head to press against the fence. The rotten wood wouldn't keep the animal at bay for very long. One of them would die today. And she didn't intend to be the one.

Amy raised the gun to her shoulder and aimed, her finger on the trigger. "I realize this is difficult for you, and it gives me no pleasure to upset you, but the issue really needs to be settled."

From Leeann:
No Safe Haven by Kim & Kayla Woodhouse, Ch 14 and Ch 29

They'd made good progress today, but Cole wanted to make it back to the crash site.

If they didn't they might not know what had caused the plane to burst into flames and fall into the side of the mountain. So many reporters, so many treasure-hunters and wanna-be detectives taking souvenirs from the plane meant that critical evidence would soon disappear.

The problem was getting to where the plane went down. A storm had blown into the area in the last couple of hours, and all helicopters were grounded. She could hike in, but that would take hours. She could take a snowmobile, but apparently all the snowmachines had been rented by the newshounds.

Cole sighed. Seemed the only option was that obnoxious Mr. Carmichael who owned the dog team. She'd have to grovel and apologize, no doubt, for suggesting his team of mutts shouldn't eat dog food, they should be dog food. Oh, she hated having to say she was sorry.

Well, there was nothing to be done about the situation. So grovel she would.

She stomped to Carmichael's shack and pounded on the door. He seemed to take a lot of pleasure in treating her like a delicate porcelain vase, but she would not act like one. She was a strong woman who knew her own mind and could make her own way. And she would let him know.

The door swung inward, and Carmichael filled the doorway, casting a ten-foot shadow across the yard. "Ah, Miss Adams."

"Cole."

His brow drew down. Apparently he was easily confused. "Miss Cole?"

She sighed. "No. I don't like effeminate titles that minimize a person. Call me Cole."

His brow relaxed and he gestured her in. "Come in, Cole."

She tapped the snow from her boots before stepping inside the cabin. Glancing around, she noted the plaid curtains, the homemade quilt on the single bed, and the order in the small space. Everything in its place, and a place for everything. She decided the guy wasn't all bad.

"Have a seat, Miss--uh, Cole."

She shook her head. "Haven't got time. Need to get to the crash site. Need a dog team." Even to her own ears, her voice sounded gruff and demanding. She attempted to soften her words. "Please."

Carmichael smiled, his eyes sparkling in the light from the fire. He stared at her for several long minutes before nodding. "We can do that."

"You can send a bill to the NTSB."

He shook his head and sat down. "No can do. Cash on the barrel head. Payment in full before I harness the team."

"That's not how--"

"The government works." He finished her sentence for her.

She hated when men did that.

But he wasn't done. "Not how I work." He held out a hand, palm up. "Cash."

"How much?"

"Two hundred."

She sucked in a breath. She didn't have that kind of cash. And he knew she didn't. What game was he playing? She'd call his bluff. "Thank you for your time. I'll get someone else."

"There isn't anyone else. You know it, and I know it. So what's the problem?"

Next to apologizing, she also hated looking inept. "I don't have the money."

He stood, looming over her, filling every spare inch of the small room. "Maybe we can make a trade."

Bile and anger rose in her throat, and she clenched her fists at her side. "I've shot men for less."

He stepped back, blinking, nostrils flaring. "I didn't mean what you thought I mean."

"Then what did you mean?" Now she felt foolish. Number three on her hate list.

"I need your help. You scratch my back and I'll scratch yours."

The idea of scratching what was undoubtedly a broad, well-muscled back, probably covered in fine, silky hair, had its appeal, but not here, and not now. She swallowed, pushing those crazy thoughts down. "Such as?"

"My sister, Jenna, needs a doctor. She's sick. If I take you to the crash site, you've got to agree to fly her out to the coastal hospital."

Cole considered the barter then nodded. Seemed like the least she could do. "What's she sick with?"

He shrugged. "Don't know for sure. Fever, cough."

"Where is she?"

He quirked his head toward a door Cole hadn't noticed before. "In there."

Cole crossed the room and opened the door. A woman lay in a cot, a quilt pulled to her chin. She entered the dim room, and an odor hit her nose immediately. Like a hunk of moose meat left out in the sun. Or a raccoon that died beneath a cabin.

Rotting flesh.

She studied the outline of the woman's body under the covers. One leg was markedly shorter than the other. Cole walked to Jenna's side. "What is this about, Mr. Carmichael?"

Day 7 -- Write a letter to yourself telling you what you need to improve in the coming 6 months.

Dear Donna:

I trust this letter finds you in good spirits and well. I know I haven't written in some time, and truth be told, I've held off as I didn't want to upset you in any way. I know you have enough on your hands and your mind, and don't need anything else added to your concerns.

However, I've watched and listened and can hold my tongue no longer. Self, you need to stop worrying about getting the outline perfect, and focus instead on the writing. Imagine if Mark Twain had said he couldn't write Huckleberry Finn unless he knew every character's complete backstory before he wrote word one? He'd never have written this fine book which people enjoy so much.

That said, I've come up with some suggestions to help you get over this particular shortcoming. No more notepads except the one you're writing the story on. No more scribbles in the margins about checking on this or that. No more getting up at midnight to sharpen your pencils, and no more skipping your midday meal so you can afford ink. Think of the time and money you'll save if you simply sit and write. I believe if you follow my suggestions, you will see a huge improvement in your writing output in as little as six months.

And while you're doing that, please see fit to make the time to write to me. I'm getting lonely out here, not knowing your news.

All my love,

Me.

Hi Leeann:

Long time, no talk. I would have used email but the Internet has been down here because of the snow storms. And I know how much you hate texting. I just don't get it, a modern gal like you.

Well, you told me if I ever had something on my chest, I was to get it off and tell you what I thought. And I've been doing a lot of thinking over the past month, what with the power off and no Internet.

Amazing how much time I've had to haul firewood and melt snow for water when I can't play Solitaire or get on Facebook.

Which is what I want to talk to you about. You need more of a presence online. More friends and twitters. More fun stuff. More reasons for people to check out your website and follow your blog. You are cute and perky and all the things your BFF Donna isn't. And don't worry, she says that all the time, so it's not like I'm putting her down. Just repeating her own words. At any rate, you need to focus on this stuff for like the next six months or so.

So try it and let me know how it's going. I'll check back again if I don't hear from you.

Knock 'em dead, girlfriend!

Me.

Day 8 -- Rewrite a fairy tale from the bad guy's point of view.

From Donna:

Cinderella's Wise Step-Mother

Once upon a time there was a step-mother who married a man with a lazy daughter. The lazy daughter didn't want to help out around the house, and taunted the step-mother's two daughters because they had big feet. Many nights the lazy daughter went to bed without supper because of her disobedience.

When the prince sent an invitation for all the young women in the kingdom to come to a fancy ball, the step-mother told the lazy daughter that she could go if she did her chores. But she didn't, so the lazy daughter wasn't allowed to go to the dance. But she snuck out, and the step-mother chased her all the way to the palace. When she saw the lazy daughter dancing with the prince, the step-mother marched up to them.

"Do you want to marry a woman who won't do as she's told?"

The prince shook his head. "Of course not."

The step-mother grabbed the lazy daughter by the arm. "Then you won't want this one." She marched the lazy daughter back to their house. "Next time, maybe you'll do your chores."

And so the lazy daughter learned a valuable lesson, and thanked her step-mother for not letting her get away with being lazy. And later on she married a poor woodcutter and had fourteen children, and taught them not to be lazy, too.

From Leeann:

I Had Red Riding Hood for Dinner

Once upon a time, there was a little girl who lived in the woods. This little girl had a cloak with a red hood, and she would pull the hood down over her face and run around the woods, scaring all the animals.

Finally, after many years of hiding from the little girl, the animals went to the Big Bad Wolf to ask for help. He was wise and kind, and often took in orphaned animals until a new home could be found for them. At least, that's what he told the animals. Sometimes when they found a home for the orphans, the wolf couldn't find them. A lot of the orphans ran away, it seems.

At any rate, the animals didn't know what to do about this little girl. The Big Bad Wolf said he would invite her to his house for dinner and talk to her. The animals thought this was a good idea. So he invited her to come to his house for dinner.

When she stepped in his door, she pulled the hood down over her face and shook her cloak at him. "Boo! Hoo!"

The wolf just stood there. "Is that how you scare the animals?"

She raised her hood. "Yes. Aren't you scared?"

He sneered at her. "I'm not sure. Do it again."

She did, and he gobbled her up in a flash.

Later, when the animals came to tell the Big Bad Wolf that the little girl was nowhere to be seen, they found him lounging in front of the fireplace, his belly full. He just smiled at them and said, "She came for dinner."

Day 9 -- Turn on your TV. Write down the first line that you hear and write a story based on it.

From Donna: "I thought you'd never get here"

Maddie glared at her twin brother Matt. "You were supposed to pick me up an hour ago."

Matt dug his toe into the dust at his feet, his cheeks coloring. "Shucks, Maddie. Sometimes a man just wants time to hisself."

She wasn't letting him off the hook so easily. "And when you act like a man, I'll treat you like one."

"I just wanted to--"

"I know exactly where you were. Out behind the mercantile playing dice with the boys." Her fists dug into her hips. "How much did you lose this time?"

"Not much."

"How much?"

"Two dollars."

Her breath caught in her throat as she eyed the sacks and bundles at her feet. That two dollars was to pay for their provisions for the next month.

Now what was she going to do?

(In this idea, Maddie and Matt are trying to run their father's ranch by themselves. As we can see, Maddie is the responsible one, while Matt still has some maturing to do."

From Leeann: "It's all right, it's okay, really doesn't matter if you're old and gray."

Carolyn ran her fingers through her short-cropped mop, eying the wrinkles and the silver mixed in with the brown hair. Sure, it was fine for them to sing about age not mattering.

But the letter on her dresser and the month's severance told a different story.

She was fifty-six, out of a job, and nobody was calling her to work for them.

"Face it, girl. You are desperate." She glanced at the flyer she'd found taped to her door the previous day. Make $1000 a week from home. Minimal investment required.

Maybe the Big Guy upstairs had heard her prayers after all.

(In this idea, Carolyn has just been let go from her job and doesn't see how she's going to survive. In an effort to make some money quick, she invests her money with a business that scams her. When the con artist is found dead, Carolyn is suspected of killing him)

Day 10:
Go sit in a public place and eavesdrop on a conversation. Turn what you hear into a short love story (no matter how much you have to twist what they say).
From Donna:

"I don't like this."

Margaret sighed. Sometimes seven-year-olds could be exasperating. "I know you don't, but it's not your decision to make."

"But Mommy, you have me." Carl's bottom lip jutted out. "Daddy said I'm the man of the house."

"But I love Mr. Fowler. We want to get married."

"I don't love him. He's not Daddy."

"I'd like to be your new Daddy." Joe Fowler stood in the doorway of the small cabin. "And won't you be a special boy, with two daddies."

Carl's eyes narrowed as he considered this prospect. "Two daddies?"

Joe nodded. "Sure. I can't do such an important job all on my own. I'll need your first Daddy's help."

Carl smiled and jumped down from his chair, running to grab Joe around the legs. "I like that idea." He turned to his mother. "It's okay, Mommy. Let's get married."

From Leeann:

"Today is the last straw. I can't take it any more." Heather twirled her straw in her soda. "If he doesn't stop, he has to go."

Paul knew how Heather felt. He'd had problems with Jake before. Not in the same way, of course, or to the same degree, but he knew. "Nobody would blame you."

Heather peered at him over the glass. "Still, it seems cruel. I mean, when we got together, we both believed it was forever."

"But things change."

She shook her head. "I don't know. Maybe I'm wrong about him."

Paul was losing her to her guilt and conscience, and if that happened, Jake would stay. In which case, there'd be no room for him in Heather's life. He couldn't let that happen. "I'm sure Jake could find someone else to love him."

"Maybe. But not the way I do."

"Maybe not. But then again, you never know."

She slapped the table with an open hand. "I never knew that getting rid of a stinking dog that eats my furniture would be so hard."

Day 11:

Write the acknowledgments page that will be placed in your first (next?) published book, thanking all the people who have helped you along the way.

From Donna:

Many thanks to:

First and foremost, the One True God, creator of all, for this story
and the privilege of writing it under His direction;
Terrie Wolf, my awesome agent;
Patrick, my equally awesome husband;
Kristian Dewar and Sydney Leube, Fort Bridger Historical Site;
Gary Lancaster, Pony Express Colorado;
Kay Rossiter, Uinta County Museum, Evanston, WY;
Pony Express Museum, St. Joseph, Missouri;
Marysville Pony Express Museum, Marysville, Kansas;
Scottsbluff Historical Site; and
Mary, Sandy, Anita, and Lynn
for your encouragement and help in developing the concept

From Leeann:

Many thanks to:

First and foremost, the One True God, who let me transcribe His story;
Terrie Wolf, who believed in my story before I did;
Patrick, who supported me through this process;
My critique group through HIS Writers and my local chapter of ACFW

Day 12 -- Gather everything you've written over the previous 11 days. Pick your favorite. Edit it, polish it and either try to get it published or post it on the Web to share with the world. Be proud of yourself and your work.

Day 13--write at least 100 words about something that you love

From Donna:

I love to write. Now, I know that's not 100 words, yet, so I need to keep going. I love to write because I can explore issues and problems without confronting them directly. I don't have to deal with these issues and problems. My characters get to do that. So I can see how someone else would handle that same issue or problem, leaving me free to view the outcome from the outside, kind of like watching fish in a fish bowl. If I don't like the outcome, I don't need to adopt it as my own. I just need to make it believable.

From Leeann:

I love to write, too. Except I have a completely different reason. Donna is an introvert, and sometimes it can be difficult to get her out to meet new people. So I solve that problem by creating these new people in my head and then putting them down on paper. These new people are my new best friends, and Donna doesn't have to complain about the phone ringing off the hook or people traipsing in and out of the house--they come to visit when I sit in front of the computer, they go home when I type "the end"--except, of course, they never really leave, do they?

Day 14-- Start your story with: "He glanced at his watch impatiently..."

From Donna:

He glanced at his watch impatiently. Would the train never arrive. Walter scanned the track leading to the horizon. Maybe she wouldn't be on the train at all. Maybe she'd decided not to come.

What had he been thinking, sending his life savings of thirty dollars to a woman he'd never met.

And asking her to come to Eastonville, Wyoming to be his wife?

He must have been out of his mind.

Walter checked his watch again, the pocket watch he'd inherited from his daddy. One minute later than the last time he looked at the fine filigree minute hand set against the mother-of-pear face.

A low moan reached his ears. He looked up. A small cloud lay over the track where the iron rails met the blue sky in the midst of the brown prairie grass that rolled like the waves on the ocean. At least, that's what he'd been told. He hadn't never seen the ocean.

The train was right on time.

The big question was: would she be on the train?

From Leeann:

He glanced at his watch impatiently. Ryan Cole shifted in place, pressing his back against the brick wall, trying to ease the cramp that started in his calf and threatened to work its way up his thigh. He was getting too old for this kind of work.

A bead of sweat trickled down his forehead and dripped into his left eye, obscuring his vision for a heartbeat and a half. He shook his head, sending drops of sweat flying in all directions.

To his left, a second sharpshooter squinted against the hot July sun. To his right, his tactical commander, a man younger than Ryan's own thirty-three by at least six years, listened to a voice crackling in his earwig. The man nodded once, shook his head twice, then spit on the ground.

Looked like he didn't like whatever instructions he'd been given.

Ryan winced, willing the cramp to go away, praying he wouldn't have to straighten his leg or draw attention to his discomfort by moving out of position.

He was getting too old for this kind of work.

Takeaway: We write even when we don't add words to our manuscript. Writing is much more than mere words on a page.

Pulled in Many Directions

A blog is due. Contest entries to be judged. Editing due for a client. Writing in my own book. After all, maybe it's NaNoWriMo month. The next book to be plotted. A book release. An online course to complete. A deadline I kind of forgot to put on my schedule. Not to mention all those pesky things called Life that call to be done, like laundry, dinner, and sleep.

I'm sure none of you have ever been in this situation, where there are too many demands and not enough hours. Just for fun--or was it madness--I listed all the things I need to do, and the time it will take to complete them, and I came up with 42 hours.

So how do we fit all these demands into our lives? Here's what I do (keep in mind I work from home. If you hold down an outside job, you will need to tailor this to fit your schedule):

a. Make a list of everything you need to do.
b. Guesstimate how much time it's going to take you to do it.
c. Make a note if there is a deadline date. For example, the contest judging has to be completed by a certain date.
d. Assign dates to each item of when you plan to do it. For tasks that take more than 6 hours, assign two dates, preferably back-to-back days so you can get a sense of accomplishment and not lose time and energy in bringing yourself up to speed.
e. DO NOT give yourself any more than 6 hours of work per day. This will give you enough time to deal with other things, like eating, email, and sleep. Stuff always comes up. Plan on it.
f. Cross off each item with flourish.
g. If you do something that isn't on your list, write it down and cross it off.

I know, there are some of you rolling your eyes at the idea of a list. But if you feel like your life is totally out of control, maybe now is the time to try something different.

Takeaway: There is nothing wrong with being badge oriented, or list-driven, or rewards-focused.

Exercises:

1. Make a list. Go ahead. Try it.
2. Forget everything you wrote on the list. That' s what the list is for.
3. Cross off each item with a big marker, or a skinny pencil, or a yellow highlighter. Whatever you need to feel you' ve accomplished something today.
4. Got on to the next item.

THE WRITING JOURNEY

Why Digital First?

There is much discussion in the publishing world about whether e-Publishing is "real publishing" or not. And it seems that the answer to that question depends on which side of the publishing desk one is sitting. With the marked growth in Amazon, Nook, Smashwords, and other e-publishers, "digital first" has become a way for independent authors to publish their books, get their names in front of readers, and create a selling history in the hopes of attracting a traditional publisher.

Here are the steps I took to e-publish my first two books.

1. Polish the book--regardless whether the book is available in print or digitally, put your best foot forward. Readers know bad writing, and they won't buy another book with your name on it, even if they only have to pay 99 cents for it. And they'll tell all their friends not to buy.
2. Do the legal stuff--if you don't have a business name, set one up. I set up a separate entity with a name that looked like a publishing company, because e-publishing is still publishing.
3. Copyright is the right thing to do--register your book. Wait until you have the final version, because once you upload the manuscript, any change made to the title, author, or body of the book will require you to register--and pay for--another copyright. You can do this at www.Copyright.gov
4. Buy the ISBN--this is the unique identifier for your book. Even an e-Book needs an ISBN. The good news is that you can use the same ISBN for each digital version of the book. You buy these at www.Bowker.com . I bought the (gulp) package of 100 ISBN's. I dream big.
5. Decide where you want to release the book--Amazon.com is the largest e-Book retailer, but there are others. Nook and Smashwords are two I chose in addition to Amazon. If you work on a Mac, you can also publish to the Apple store. Each venue has advantages and disadvantages. Smashwords lets

you put out a coupon. All of these venues will allow you to upload the manuscript in advance of the actual launch date. Try different options for different books and see what works best for you.

6. Design a cover--I made the decision early to design my own cover. I took high quality photographs, about 20 of them, from different angles, positioning the elements in the photos in different positions, then chose the one I liked best, using Photoshop to design the cover. I plan to use the same cover on the print version when that time comes.
7. Tell everybody--create a group in your email program of everybody who might be remotely interested in your book or will tell others about your book. Then send an exciting call-to-action email to them.

Hopefully, all this hard work will result in a best seller and the phone will start ringing from publishers. But even if it doesn't, you will have the satisfaction of answering in the affirmative when someone asks, "A writer? Are you published?"

Takeaway: Anybody can publish a book, but it takes work to publish a book worth reading.

Exercises:

1. Look at the books you've written which are not published. Which one are you willing to release to the world first? Second? Third?
2. Is there a series you'd like to see published? Perhaps a short story collection? A devotional book? Figure out how much work will be required to get it ready.
3. Research the copyright requirements and ISBN number cost. Decide how much you're willing to invest, then DO IT!

Never Enough Time--or is there?

It seems there is never enough time to do all the things I want to do. With seven days in a week, twenty-four hours in a day, seems like I should have lots of spare time. I don't suppose anyone else finds the same problem? No, I didn't think so.

My idea of a perfect week would begin with Sunday. Some awesome praise and worship, a soul-stirring message, and a couple of hours of fellowship. Not more than that. I'm an introvert, and more than two hours and I'd be exhausted. For you extroverts, party on until midnight!

On Monday, I'd like to get all those administrative things like paperwork and laundry done by 10:00 so I'd have the rest of the day to write. Doesn't happen. Could if I got up earlier.

On Tuesday, Write. That's the day I go to a write out from 10:00 to noon at a coffee shop with friends. No write out in your area? Start one. I did. I went to the write out for a year before anyone else joined me. No shame in that. I got a lot of writing done.

On Wednesday, carry on the flow from Tuesday and write. Sometimes that happens. Often it doesn't. Lots of times the writing from Tuesday raised questions and I spend a lot of time researching. Or planning research trips because I discovered I didn't know as much about something as I need so I can write about it.

On Thursday, that's my "work" day, the day I do my "other job". Usually a full day of listening to other people's mistakes and problems (I proofread legal transcripts). Honestly, so many sad stories that I don't want to think about writing.

On Fridays, that's the day we give to our local food bank. Lots of people -- so exhausting for this introvert.

Saturdays are my "free" day. I usually use Saturdays to catch up on tasks I let slip during the week. Sometimes I write, the next week I might do something around the house, like canning, or cleaning, or ironing. Remember the laundry I did Monday? Mending and ironing to be done.

My week is full. And I'm sure your weeks are full, too. But if we want to be writers, we need to make time to write. We won't find time but we can compress certain activities to expand our available time. We can drop some tasks from our schedule completely, or we can delay some things to allow us time to write.

Every day for the next month, I challenge you to make an extra hour a day to write. Not to think about writing, not to plot, not to research, but to write. Call me crazy, but once a year I take a leave of absence from television and spend that time writing. You can choose to go a little easier on yourself: no television until you write for at least an hour. Don't watch television? Think of other ways to put together an extra 60 minutes a day. Like doing one less load of laundry. Or have one of the kids do the folding. Instead of reading before you go to bed, write.

Takeaway: We can live on never enough time, or we can decide to make the time to do the things that are important to us.

Exercises:

1. Go through your calendar and find those pockets of time you can divert to writing.
2. Be honest about the ways you spend your time: Pinterest, email, Facebook. Limit those activities to one time a day.
3. Be ready with a story outline and character sketches so when you sit to write, you really do write.

Writing Under Deadline

In the writing world, there are two kinds of deadlines: the ones imposed by others; and the ones imposed by you. The deadlines that others set for you in your writing might include a contest entry date; a critique group submission due date; a time frame for the submission of a proposal and first three chapters to an editor or agent following a contact at a writing conference such as the ACFW National Conference; a request for a full manuscript; the acceptance and signing of a contract; first draft approval; intermediate revisions; and final revisions prior to publication. Each one of these deadlines is critical to the process of writing, of keeping everything flowing, and of ultimately achieving the goal, whether that be winning a contest, being a productive member of a critique group, acquiring an agent, or publication.

And there are the self-imposed deadlines, the ones you set for yourself. And whether you realize it or not, you set deadlines every day, some that are related to writing and some that are not. For example, you get up at a certain time of the day. You have set the deadline on how long you're going to spend sleeping. If you have children, you get them off to school. Each deadline, while not specifically adding words or pages to your work in process, is a practice at meeting a deadline.

So how do you set self-imposed writing deadlines when there is no agent, no editor, no promise of an advance or a royalty looming over your head?

Treat your writing seriously, or you won't set goals. Look at the book you're working on, look at your schedule--because face it, we all have a life outside of writing--and determine how much time you can spend on writing, and how much you can reasonably expect to get done in that time. For example, I was working on a novella. When I started the book, I was excited about the story, excited about where the characters were going. I figured this book would just leap out of my mind, through my fingers, and into the computer.

That didn't happen. I was so convinced I could have this done in no time that that's exactly what I spent writing--no time. Suddenly the story was boring, and the laundry looked more interesting.

So around the middle of the third month of not writing, I decided enough was enough. I set a goal for the end of the month to have the story finished. I was about 20,000 words from the end. Still didn't happen. Seemed I had all the time in the world. For other things. So I buckled down and started writing seriously three days before the end of the month. I wrote 2,500 words the first day, 1,500 words the second, and 4,500 words the final day. I didn't quite make my goal because the story wasn't finished. But I was on a roll. Spending every day in the story made the story more real to me. And setting a deadline made me feel like I real writer.

Did I set a bad deadline? No. The problem was I wasn't serious enough about the work required.

Should I simply dump the story and move on? No. Writing every day has kept me in the story and opened some new plot points and back story points, and that's exciting for me.

How do I learn from this experience? I won't take the next deadline for granted. I will treat the deadline as if a contract, an advance, or publication depend on it.

Takeaway: I will act like I am a writer under a deadline imposed by someone else.

Exercises:

1. What work in process would you like to finish?
2. Take out the story, read through it to ground yourself again, and set a deadline.
3. Write every day, even if it's only for a few minutes, to keep yourself grounded in the story.

Doing What You Hate to Do

Writing is such a love-hate relationship. No matter who you talk to, you'll find someone who loves to do what you dislike, and who hates what you love. And not loving every aspect of the writing journey is okay. I give you permission to dislike something. But that doesn't mean you are now free to make your own rules, or to break the established rules, or to produce an inferior product. Perhaps the insight and information below will ease you through the 'dislikes' into the The End.

For example, some people hate plotting. They say it stifles the creativity, puts them in a box where they don't feel free to write. For me, I love plotting. And I'm not going to say you must plot or you absolutely don't need to plot. The truth is, even those who say they don't plot really do – in some dark part of their brain, they know where their story is going and how they're going to get to the end. Plus, just about every publisher wants a synopsis, so even if you don't plot in advance, you'll do a plot outline at some point.

I make a simple chart with however many chapters I think will be in the book, and I write a few words about each scene. Here's a sample from a novel I wrote, "No Accounting for Murder", book 1 in a mystery series, which was recently published in eBook format on Amazon, NOOK, and Smashwords:

1. Introd uction Carly Turnquist Town of Bear Cove Mention past mystery	2 Introduce nudist colony	3 Introduce mayor's mystery; introduce secondary characters	4 Numbered company; missing money and time constraint	5- 1st inciting incident: Receives fax job offer; mayor won't talk to her
6 Receive fax threat in response to turning down job; drive to Denise's; accident	7 Find out brake lines cut; meet police officer	8 examine bank statements; see mayor; Nearly pushed in harbor	9 continue investigatin g; call to bank about numbered company	10 – 2nd inciting incident: Introduce principal; meeting; get go-ahead to keep on looking for missing money; mayor dead
11 – Point of no return: Family threatened	12 Mike agrees to help; talk to police officer; look at bank statements;	13 Return to Bear Cove; talk to Susan; introduce mayor's gambling	14 Set up plant at post office; pull together notes; talk to	15 coroner says mayor's death murder; evidence

	was mayor's death suicide/accident/murder?	problem?	mechanic; introduce development and dislike of mayor	mayor being blackmailed; get another threat
16– talk to mechanic about mayor's car; Mike called away to client	17 Carly calls police officer to check mileage on mayor's car; Carly talks to real estate agent/friend	18 – Crisis Carly talks to suspects; she falls unconscious in house while Mike is gone	19 – Climax Carly taken to hospital; sets up news story for killer to try again	20 – Resolution Killer tries again and is caught; mayor's wife returns stolen money; set up for next book.

As you can see, this outline is fairly open, not much detail, and leaves lots of room for the characters and my imagination to weave a story, while still resolving all the plot lines and keeping the action moving forward.

Another thing I often hear from writers is that they hate to revise. Okay. I confess. Me too. I would like to just sit and write the stories and let someone else do the revising. But the truth is, if I didn't revise, I wouldn't learn what works and what doesn't. I wouldn't understand the rules, which ones to break, and which ones to follow even if I don't agree with them. I'd keep writing in the same style, and I'd probably find my voice wouldn't change with the story.

So how do I overcome this dislike? I make lists and tackle one thing at a time. I write down my characters' physical traits and check that I've carried those through the book so my heroine doesn't start out with blue eyes and end up with green ones. I do the same with my setting, treating it like a character so I don't have Main Street crossing Water Street in one place and running parallel in another.

I have a list of 'weasel words', and I do a search one by one until I've eliminated most of them. Sometimes that requires simply taking the word out, or changing it. And sometimes I have to – gulp – rewrite a sentence. But the writing is always better for the investment of time. My list of weasel words has changed over time. I've come to recognize that when I'm lazy, I fall into bad writing patterns, but here are a few of them:

It – describe what it is instead of saying "it"
Almost
Just
Just about
Nearly
Suddenly
Well
Wow
It goes without saying
It was obvious
Obviously
And – at the beginning of a sentence
All –ly adverbs
Anywhere there are two adjectives together – choose the better one, or choose another one

The third complaint I've heard is about critique groups. Seems some writers have gotten into groups that just didn't work for them. Or, most often, it's a difference of opinion between the writer and one particular person in the group. That's okay. As believers, we're called to love everybody – we don't have to like them or even do what they tell us. How do I overcome differences of opinion from my critique group? I take each submission, consider who it's from, and make changes according to the purpose of my story and my voice. If I have one person who says they don't understand something, but the rest seem fine, I don't make the change. But, if more than one person says they don't understand, or the sentence is clunky, or the word is unfamiliar, I look at making a change. With an uncommon or foreign word, perhaps I can describe the object. For example, in another novel, "My Surrendered Heart", I say the rider threw the mochila over the saddle. Then I go on to describe: "The rider mounted his horse, effectively anchoring the two sets of saddlebags joined by a single sheet of leather beneath him." Anybody who knows Pony Express history knows what a mochila is, and anybody who doesn't, now has a picture of what it looks like. And the fact is, even if they don't have a completely accurate picture, it doesn't matter, so long as they understand the rider sits on it and it carries the mail.

Writing can be a lonely prospect, an intimidating process, and a questionable pursuit. But if you are called to write, if you are prepared to persevere, then you can become a writer who, while you may not enjoy every aspect of the process, will at least do what you need to make the story the best it can be.

Takeaway: Writing well is its own reward

Exercises:

1. Go through one of your works in process and search for "weasel" words. Use my list if you don't have one of your own.
2. Prepare a plotting chart for this same novel and see if there are any gaps in the story.
3. Do some research about local or online critique groups. Find one that fits your schedule and contact them about joining. No group nearby? Start one.

Those Lazy, Hazy Days of Summer

I keep promising myself that one of these years, I'm going to enjoy summer. Instead of spending the months of June, July, and August cooped up indoors writing and revising and researching, I'm going to spend the time in a mountain retreat, on the front veranda, surrounded by trees and a babbling brook. Writing and revising and researching.

So I guess the truth is, it isn't the work that I resent as much as the being indoors. Seems such a waste of great weather not to be outside enjoying it. I don't have any problems staying indoors in the winter. I am not a fan of cold and snow. But summer ...

And then I heard those words from my agent, Terrie Wolf, that every writer longs to hear. "Take some time off. You've been working hard lately. You deserve a rest."

My mind raced. Which mountain did I want to go to? Which tree would I sit beneath? Which babbling brook would sing to me, inspire me as my fingers flew across the keyboard?

Nothing came to mind.

Okay, maybe I don't need a mountain. Maybe I need a cruise. Sitting on the deck, the sun warming me from the outside, my story plot heating up inside. Perfect.

Except I'm prone to seasickness.

Okay, how about a quaint bed and breakfast retreat in a sleepy little town. Where do I want to set my next book? Let's go there.

I'm drawing a blank.

And then I realize my problem. It's not that I don't have any ideas of what to write next. I do. Dozens of ideas. It isn't that I can't choose a mountain or a town or a cruise -- my problem is I like to write in my office in the basement. I have a peaceful moss green paint on the walls along with peaceful pictures of the outdoors. I have a great desk and a comfy chair. I can have music on in the background, or not. I can stop and pop in a load of laundry or stir dinner in the crock pot. Or not.

And so, despite my agent's advice, I'm going to stay home. And write. And outline. And research.

Sure, I'll go out once in a while and see what I'm missing. Sunshine. Flowers. Heat.

I'll take pictures and keep writing.

Maybe I'll write a summer story. That way, I don't miss anything.

Takeaway: It's not all about where you write, but that you do write.

Exercises:

1. Make a writing date for yourself. In ink. On your calendar or schedule or whatever you use to keep track of things. Be reasonable. If you aren't already in the habit of writing every day, schedule in every other day. If you work a full-time job, don't commit to writing for three hours in the evening or all day Saturday. Instead, commit to spending twenty minutes at your computer with the email turned off.
2. If you struggle with finding time, make time. Get up twenty minutes earlier. Go to bed twenty minutes later. Don't watch any television in the evening until you've spent your twenty minutes at the computer.
3. Pretend you have a deadline. Maybe not for a full book. Try setting a deadline for a chapter. Call a writing friend and tell him you commit to having a chapter written by __________. Tell your friend to hold you accountable. Then sit down and write.

Memories and Memoirs

My father had an interesting life story as well as an interesting family story. When he approached me to write these two stories down, I took him up on the offer. He understood that his story wasn't unique, yet the people were. His goal was to get the details down for the family as a keepsake. I saw something bigger.

His tale of growing up in a small town in the 1930's and 1940's would make an interesting book in and of itself, were it not for the well-kept--and not-so-well-kept--secrets that abound in every family and every town. The question became how to present the story.

Memories can make a great foundation for any book. For example, you might recall an incident from your childhood where a neighbor boy steals your bike, and your father makes you retrieve it. I was about four, and that actually happened. So I made that part of one of the back story for my character, Betsy Rollins, a feisty rancher woman in northern Colorado, in the first book of a series I'm working on. The real incident happened far from its fictional setting, but that doesn't matter--this is the kind of event that could happen anywhere.

Another memory I have yet to weave into a tale--perhaps I'll bring it out in my current project--is of my father and my mother's father eating cherries and spitting the pits against the side of our mobile home to see who can spit the furthest. That in itself is a treasure, but next I recall my mother's mother coming to the door to chastise them. But when she turns away, she is smiling.

Did that really happen that way? I don't know, but that's my story and I'm sticking to it.

Memories can make wonderful fodder for stories, but when they are bolstered by facts and details written at the time, these memories take on a whole new authority--that of a memoir. And my father provided me with a box of contemporaneous and near-contemporaneous records. I have the cash books from his father's general store with notations on the happenings of the day, including births, deaths, marriages, suicides, vacations, operations, and who came to visit. I also have letters written thirty or forty years after the fact that refer to some of the events mentioned in the cashbooks.

Structuring a memory-based memoir poses some problems that are not unique to stories, and include:

1. Who is the story about? Figure out who your main characters are, and what you want the reader to know about them.
2. Who is telling the story? I have decided that to get into the essence of the characters, his biological mother will tell her story, and he will tell his stories. Because he has two stories: the one of his growing up years, and the one of his reunion with his half-brothers and –sisters.
3. Where to start? Memoirs have a pattern of starting when the character is born and going through, following a chronological order. I chose to start his birth mother's story on the day after her mother is buried, a turning point in her life. I use flashbacks, then move forward in leaps and bounds, often skipping months or years. In my father's story, I start where he learns that his sister is his mother. And in the third part, where he meets his biological father's children, I go forward from their first meeting.
4. How much truth? So much time has gone past that a completely accurate retelling of the story is impossible. Memories fade, people die, and the internet doesn't have all the information. The best you can do is research the setting and the people, then go forward from there. Fill in the gaps so long as it's possible the event might have happened. For example, since my grandfather owned a general store, and I have some inventory notations, I can mention various goods sold in the shop. However, he never went to France, and to say that he did, would be wrong. I could say he went ice skating on the harbor ice, because he probably did at some point in his life.
5. What about if the truth hurts someone? I am writing this story using the real names of the people involved. I will likely change those names before I submit it anywhere, but for right now, it's

> easier to keep the names straight by using their real names. I am writing this story to record a period of time in my family's history--and in the town's history--that shouldn't be lost. My goal is to show these people in the best light possible, to show they can and did change for the better, even if they didn't. But that's the fiction part of the story. And I am sprinkling in enough fiction so that this is not a biography.

Memories told in a memoir style is simply another way to tell a story. You want the reader to say, "This could have happened just like that." The reader understands that the way you string the story together is for the benefit of the story, not of the history. We are not striving to rewrite history with our memory stories; in fact, we keep the facts alive by dressing them in another suit of clothes.

Do you have an interesting story from your family that would make a good foundation for a book? Perhaps the story is simply a nugget and would be good for back story, like my bicycle story. Or perhaps the history is deep and wide enough to propel an entire novel.

Takeaway: There is no such thing as a boring story when a storyteller strings the words together.

Exercises:

1. Write down some memories from your childhood, or family stories you recall. How could these be used as back story for a character or as the basis for action in a book?
2. Go through an old family album and ask your parents or someone who knows about the pictures and the stories behind them.
3. Visit a museum and pretend the people in the old pictures were your parents or grandparents. What would their stories be?

THE CRAFT OF WRITING

Paint Yourself Into a Book

Living in an old house provides lots of opportunity for devising plots, particularly when the task at hand is painting a room. As I slathered yet another coat of paint over the neon blue bedroom walls, I got to thinking about how painting and writing require similar processes.

When painting a room, the first step is to visualize what color you want on the walls. What color can you live with? What hue will brighten the room, make the area look more inviting, larger, perhaps? Or, if the ceilings are high, maybe you want to make the room feel more cozy. What kind of a finish you do want? Textured, faux finish, more than one color?

When you sit down to write a book, first you choose the genre, then the characters and setting. If your book is a romance, you want to choose your hero and heroine and an antagonist who will try to keep them apart. For a mystery, you will choose the problem, who did it, and then create a sleuth to find the solution. Setting includes the time period as well as geographical location. Understand your characters' goal, motivation, and conflict, and make the goal worthy of the journey.

The next step in painting a room is repairing the defects, including holes in the walls. Painting over the defects will serve merely to amplify them. A little spackle here, a little filler there, perhaps some drywall work where serious problems exist.

In your book, you want to come up with a plot line. Most often, you'll find that the first thing you think of for a plot will be the easy point. To create a compelling story, you must think beyond that first idea, and ask more "And then what?" questions. Come up with the plot, then go back and fill in the holes in the plot. Don't let your hero off the hook too easily. Make the antagonist worthy of your hero--a weak antagonist will make for a weak plot.

Unless you want your entire room the same color, you'll likely tape off areas to protect them. You may cover windows with paper, or put drop cloths on the floor and over furniture. Perhaps you're going for a striping technique, or you want to later paint a contrasting border, so you'll use tape to mark those areas. In painting, the tape marks the borders.

In writing, your outline, synopsis, and elevator pitch will keep you on track. There are few things as frustrating as sitting down to write a book and then you find out halfway through that you're not writing THAT book, but the story has taken on a life of its own and gone in a completely different direction. This usually happens because you didn't really know what the story was about before you started writing. For seat-of-the-pants writers, who will say that writing an outline steals the joy from the process, you don't have to write a ten-page outline. Even an elevator pitch, fifty words or less, can keep you on track. And for those who love to outline, the joy still emerges when a character says or does something you weren't expecting.

Finally, after all the preparation, now is the time to paint. But you can't just take a bucket of paint and throw it at the walls. No, you must have the proper tools. A good paint roller, a quality brush, perhaps a paint pan if you're using a gallon of paint, or a paint screen if you're using a five gallon bucket. Then you patiently dip, strain, and apply the paint in even strokes, one coat at a time, taking care not to miss any spots. Keep a damp rag to mop up any spills.

Writing requires tools, as well. Included in your toolkit will be something to write on, usually a computer of some sort. You will need a notepad and pen, a space where you can write, some software, and patience. You might want to set some daily or weekly goals for your writing, such as how many words or pages you want to produce. Occasionally you might want to read over what you wrote the previous day and make a few changes, the equivalent of make sure you didn't leave any bare spots. Just as with painting, writing a book takes time, patience, and commitment. Keep your outline in front of you to keep you on track. Review your characters' GMC to make sure your character is changing and moving toward their goals.

And last but not least, in the painting process, you need to clean up, including washing your tools, securely closing the paint can to protect against spills, removing the tape and dropcloths, and returning your room to a usable condition. After all, what's the point of painting the room if you don't get to enjoy it?

Once you write "the end" on your book, you still have work ahead of you. You'll want to go back and do some revisions, looking for passive voice, point of view slips, overused words, stilted dialogue, and plot holes. You'll need to check for those nasty –ly words, for consistency in character description, and for grammar and punctuation issues. Read through your book. Was this a joy or a chore? Were there some spots where the story slowed down too much? Did you give your readers a chance to catch their breath? Do you need to plant some more clues and foreshadowing? Does the story still fit the genre and market?

Sometimes I fool myself into thinking I can paint a room in a couple of hours, forgetting all the preparation and clean-up to make the job truly complete. Just as painting a room doesn't begin and end with a single brush stroke, writing a book takes a lot of preparation, process, and finish. But it can be done. I am living proof of that. I've painted many rooms and written a number of books. You can too!

Takeaway: Writing is simply painting with words.

Exercises:

1. Be willing to invest the time needed to learn the craft of writing
2. Learn the rules first before you break them, and when you break them, make sure you have a good reason.
3. Don't rush the process. Let the end come to you, not you to the end of the story.

Writing in the Midst of Life

Sometimes it seems as though we are inundated with writing helps, encouragement to write, conferences to attend, deadlines to meet. And all of those are good. They keep us focused, energized, equipped, and reminded of what's important.

But what happens when life gets in the way?

No amount of cajoling, criticism (from ourselves or someone else), or chafing will keep our backside in the chair and our fingers on the keys when something else comes between us and our story.

True, sometimes the stuff that distracts us is simply that: stuff. We could choose to ignore it, like the laundry that piles up and multiplies like bunnies in the dark recesses of our laundry room. We could choose to delegate it, like asking our spouse to make dinner tonight while we finish this chapter. We could choose to turn off the email buzzer or silence our phones for an afternoon or ask a neighbor kid to walk the dog this week.

That stuff will always be there, and we can make arrangements for that.

But what about the big stuff? The life-changing things that happen? Those events that cannot be rescheduled, must not be ignored, should not be delayed.

We all have those.

When life gets in the way of our best laid plans, here are some suggestions as to how to get through them without losing your sanity and without feeling you are abandoning your writing:

- Stop and pray. Ask the Lord whether He is trying to show you something. Maybe He has a slightly different direction for you. Maybe He misses you. Have you been making time for Him each day? Do that first, regardless of whether you "think" you need to or not.
- Stop and breathe. Think about the situation for a moment. Perhaps whatever has come up isn't as much of an emergency as you first thought. Can someone else take it on? Can you call a friend and ask them for help?

- Release the situation. If you know in your heart that this is something you must do yourself, unclench your hands from your writing and give it over to the One who called you to write in the first place. This situation might have surprised you, but it didn't surprise Him. He already had a backup plan in place.
- Do what you need to do. Sometimes we're faced with a sudden death, or an illness, or the birth of a child, or the loss of a job. All of these are life-changing events that will need your attention for a period of time. That doesn't mean you aren't a writer. That doesn't mean God is removing the calling. That doesn't mean you are stopping because the devil was right the first time and you don't have what it takes. It just means you need to do what my husband calls "a priority interrupt". In most cases, these situations will not permanently stop you from writing.
- Call in some support. Whether you're under a contract deadline, a critique group commitment, or you need to cancel your next writer's meeting, ask a friend to help communicate the situation. Ask for prayer support. Knowing a chain of prayers are being lifted on your behalf can calm the nerves and diminish the stress level.
- Keep the story in your head. No matter how stressful or hectic our lives become, there are still a few times during each day where we can focus on something other than the situation at hand. Keep a notebook with you to jot down ideas when you get a spare moment. A small digital recorder works great. Most phones and iPads come with a voice recorder. Save these thoughts wherever and whenever you can to put into place later on.
- Come back to the project with a joyful heart. Regardless of whether the interruption lasted an hour or a year, return to the project knowing that God has called you to be a writer, and that He wants you to write this story he has placed on your heart.

Takeaway: There is no shame in pausing in your writing because life throws you a curve ball.

Exercises:

1. Have you hit a roadblock in your writing because of something that's happened, or are you afraid of something? Look back over the time you haven't been writing until you get to when you stopped, and honestly assess the situation.
2. If life has gotten in the way, is it a legitimate reason not to write or an excuse?
3. If it's an excuse, resolve the problem today.

Self-Editing for Writers

I have a love-hate relationship with editing.

I love to write. Never have a problem coming up with ideas. Always got a couple of stories simmering in the back of my mind. Happy to write The End and start with plotting and planning the next book.

But editing. . .

To me, editing is like pruning a plant. I mean, I spend all that time watering and fertilizing and praying for sunshine so the plant will grow, and then you want me to cut it back? Really? What was the point of all the hours--okay, minutes, but add them up and they become hours--doing things to make the plant grow.

But deep inside, I know the plant will be healthier and happier for not having to support so many leaves and limbs. I know the flowers will be prettier, the fruit sweeter, if I will simply take my shears and lop a little off the top and a little more off the sides.

Writing is the same. We hack away on the keyboard, letting our thoughts and ideas morph into sentences that grow into paragraphs that eventually make up chapters. We turn off that internal editor so we can get the words on the page, the chapters in the right order, to be able to write The End.

And then we need to go back and self-edit before we let anybody else see our masterpiece.

When I self-edit, I look for a number of things:

1. Formatting: Does every chapter start at the same line down the page? Do I call number the chapters or spell out the numbers? Does the first line of each chapter get indented or did I choose to keep it aligned with the left margin?
2. Weasel words: we all have them. Start with some of the more common: that, sort of, obviously, it (instead, describe what it is); and weasel phrases: the point is, the last thing she needed/wanted, to her mind. You get the idea.
3. Industry standards, such as one space after punctuation at the end of a sentence; reduce internal dialog by turning it

into narrative; no more than one exclamation point per book.

4. Check for "began to", "started to"; we rarely begin to do anything. We do it.
5. Check for –ing vowels, and see if you can turn them into the more active –ed vowels. For example, Walking into the room, Sally was looking for the coffee maker. Try this: Sally walked into the room and spotted the coffee maker.

The next thing is to print out the book like it would look on the printed page (one-inch margins, right and left justified).

1. Look for white space on the page (good). If you don't have any, break up the paragraphs, add some dialog.
2. Look for "buried" dialog, where you start a paragraph with narrative, have some dialogue, and add more narrative. Change that so you don't bury the dialog. For example: Sally sipped her coffee. "Good Joe." She munched her toast. Try this: Sally washed down her mouthful of dry toast with some coffee before answering. "Good Joe."
3. Look for dialog attributions such as said, asked, whimpered, whispered, croaked, laughed, and all the rest. Change those to actions instead. For example, instead of: "I can't believe my eyes," Sally whispered. Try this: Sally leaned closer. "I can't believe my eyes."

Once you've done these steps, your work will be much more ready to send to a critique group, a trusted reader-friend, or a professional editor.

Takeaway: Self-editing is a good way to learn from our mistakes.

Exercises:

1. Choose a book you really like and read through the tenth chapter, highlighting any of the words or issues mentioned in this article. We choose the tenth chapter because quite often the first three to five chapters have been edited several times.

2. Choose one of your books and read through the first, the tenth, and the final chapter, looking for these same issues.

3. How can you learn from these mistakes so you write better?

Getting Into Character

Depending on whether you write plot-driven stories or character-driven stories determines when you start developing your characters. However, one thing is certain: you will need well-rounded characters that jump off the page for your reader if you want to keep the story flowing and interesting.

Regardless of what kind of story you write, you cannot ignore the importance of the people in the story. Even if the story is plot-driven, meaning the plot is what the story is about, you still need to have your characters interact with one another in a believable way. You might think that developing the plot and its various layers is the most important thing, which will have you leaving character development out almost entirely. Don't fall into this trap. Your readers might enjoy action and all the other elements of your plot, but they will certainly come away disappointed by your lackluster characters.

Characters are, after all, what the real story is about. And although I refer to them as "people" in this article, your story could well include non-human characters. My observations will remain largely the same whether your characters are from Boston, Botswana, an undiscovered planet in outer space, or even if they are an animal.

So how do you get into character? Or better yet, get into their head so that their voice, and not yours, comes out on the page? Every writer has their favorite method, so I will include a few of them here:

- Write a prequel story featuring your main character or characters, putting them into situations that won't appear in your novel, but that show how that person thinks and acts in various situations. For example, when I was writing my first mystery novel, No Accounting for Murder, there was a story that happened before the book began that has now become a giveaway on my website. I used that story, Roasted Bean Counters, to develop my knowledge and understanding of Carly Turnquist and her propensity to stick her nose into mysteries. You can read that story at: www.LeeannBetts.com/2.html . Or you can write sequel short stories to post on your website or other social media that include your character in other situations. I did this in John Deere Thanksgiving that features Betsy Rollins from my Box Elder Ranch series in yet another murder mystery. Enter those stories in contests or offer them for free on your website. Put them into serial form on your blog, one chapter a week. It was good enough for Sir Arthur Conan Doyle.

- Interview your character, asking all sorts of questions such as where she went to school, who broke her heart for the first time, what position did she hold amongst her siblings, what was a vivid childhood memory. I did this exercise for a character I created, Betsy Rollins, for the first in a series, Hotshot. I used a childhood memory of mine where a neighbor boy stole my bike and I went after it. He never stole from me again.
- Become your character. Maggie Magoffin is a creation of a writer friend, and she has gone so far as to create a complete persona, backstory, and publishing empire, and even dresses as Maggie for book signings and guest appearances. You can check out her activities at: http://www.maggiempublications.com/
- Post pictures around your writing area or in a binder or on your computer of what your character looks like. Include the house he lives in, the car she drives, even her family if she has one. Refer to that picture often.
- If your character exhibits a particular trait that is not familiar to you, watch a movie or read a book where one of the characters has a similar trait. For example, in one of my novels, One Moment in Time, there is a stalker. I used the book, The Psychology of Stalkers, by J. Reid Meloy. This book was so well-written that I only needed to read a couple of chapters to know all I wanted to know about my stalker's motivation.

Takeaway: Characters may be fictional, but they're real to us.

Exercises:

1. Do you have a character set in a particular time who you'd like to become from time to time? Look online for an authentic costume, or make one yourself.
2. Does one of your characters have a peculiar mannerism, such as a stammer or wears thick eye-glasses? Practice that mannerism until you can hop in and out of character at will.
3. Do you have a story with a unique character that you can enter into a contest? Do it today.

Overused Words

What are overused words? They are those words we grab when we don't want to stop and think through the scene long enough to choose the exactly correct word. They are the words that leap from our fingers onto the keyboard. And we all know how we feel about every single word we write--we love them. We don't want to delete a single one of them.

But seriously, overused words will drive an editor to toss your submission in the slush pile. A discerning reader will roll his/her eyes at the excessive use of words or phrases. And both may well end up putting your book aside for some other. And that's the last thing we want.

Because these overused words are the first we grasp on to, they tend to weaken your writing.

Particularly worrisome are weak verbs and passive voice. A weak verb is one that tells us what is happening but doesn't show us. So, for example, "He walked across the road" Would be better written as, "He stumbled across the road". "Walked" would be considered an overused word.

Another example is use of the passive voice, where the object of the sentence is not being acted on by the verb: He was running across the field. A more active way to say this would be: He raced across the field.

Often, as writers, we latch onto various words and phrases because we like the sound of the words, and then we use them over and over. One of my pet phrases is "The last thing she needed". While this may be a true statement, using that phrase more than once or even twice in a book will stand out to the editor and reader as amateur writing.

Another set of overused words are see/saw/look/watch/heard/knew/thought. If we are in deep POV, we already see and hear and know everything our POV character sees and hears and knows, so we don't need to tell the reader that the character is seeing and hearing and knowing. Take for example, "The door opened" is much more powerful than, "He saw the door open".

How to deal with overused words:

Needless to say, the easiest thing to do is not to write these words and phrases in the first place. However, that is easier said than done, particularly when you want to simply get the story down. So, when you start editing, go through your manuscript with the "find" function to identify every time one of these overused words is used, then choose another word or phrase to replace it.

Yes, this means you will go through your manuscript approximately 50 times or more. But your story will be better, and you will have the chance to look at the various sentences around these overused words and make changes then.

Words often overused:

Because we tend to use these words when we speak, using them in dialog is not so serious as using them in narrative. You don't need to completely eliminate these words--just use them sparingly and only if another word won't work better. We tend to fall back on these words when we don't take the time needed to find the exact right word.

-LY adverbs: in most cases, you can delete the word and not change the meaning of the sentence at all.

It (describe what IT is – makes the sentence more clear, avoids ambiguity, and gives you the opportunity to tell more about what IT is).

THAT (if you can take THAT out of the sentence and the sentence still makes sense, delete it).

	A bit	Absolutely
Actually	Almost	Amazing

Approached	Are you all right?	As (clauses)
Awesome	Awful/awfully	Bad
Beautiful	Because	Become/became
Began	Believe	Big
But	By	Could
Decide	Eyed/eyeing	expression
face	Feel	Felt
Fine	Found (himself/herself)	Gave
Gaze/gazed	Glanced	Good
great	Had	Happy
Have	Hear/heard	If
Interesting		Just
Knew	Know	Like
Look	Looked like	Made
Made a face	Made his/her way	Making
Maybe	Name was	Nearly
Nice	Nodded	Not certain
Not sure	Notice	Observe
Often	Quite	Reached
Really	Recalled	remembered
Said	Saw	seemed
Shook his/her head	Shot (as in shot him/her a glance)	should
Shrug/shrugged	Simply	Smell

So	Somehow	Suddenly
Taste		Then
There	Thereafter	Therefore
Think	Thought	Touched
Turned	Turned to face/to leave	Very
Was	Watched/watching	Well
When	With (prepositional phrases--don't rely on them so much)	Wondered
Would	You	

Tools to identify overused words:
This is a free service that shows not only the overused words but also offers suggestions:
http://prowritingaid.com/art/7/Find-overused-words.aspx

Articles about overused words:
http://www.barbarasloan.com/tips_overused.html
http://learnedaboutwriting.blogspot.com/2008/05/overused-words.html

Takeaway: Overused words bore the reader and distract them from your story.

Exercises:
1. Go through this list and eliminate as many as possible.
2. Add to this list those words you overuse.
3. Keep this list handy to check yourself constantly.

Conflict versus Tension

"I can't believe you said that to me." She would never have said that to him.

"Well, it's true." And sometimes the truth hurts.

"It wasn't very nice." She always tried to say nice things to people, even if they weren't completely true.

"Wasn't meant to be." Doesn't the Bible say to speak in truth?

"I'm not putting up with this." If she'd known he was going to treat her like this, she'd never have married him.

The door slams.

"Fine," he muttered. "Walk out, like you always do." Just like my mother always walked out on my father and me.

Just about every writer's conference I've attended tells us to have conflict on every page. Fine to say, more difficult to accomplish. The above passage, filled with head-hopping to make a point, is filled with conflict, every sentence venomous and filled with reactions to hurt.

While this passage has conflict, or disagreement or a failure to understand the other person's point, it is not particularly tension.

Conflict happens when two characters confront each other. Tension happens when two characters strive for opposite goals.

Conflict is fine in small doses, but this type of verbal sparring becomes tiresome. I recently watched a British historical drama, seasons one through three, one after the other. By the end of season three, I needed a break. One of the characters, a mother of five, had a hot temper, and she was forever arguing with somebody about her rights and her sacrifice for her family. I was tired of it.

Tension is more difficult to attain. We can increase tension by:

1. Upping the stakes. For example, a police officer who is looking for the bad guy, and the bad guy kidnaps our character's wife.
2. Introducing another goal our character can't have. For example, our police officer's boss takes him off the case because he's

too emotionally involved and puts him on a case involving child pornography.

3. Adding to our character's backstory. So, we find out our police officer was once addicted to kiddie porn but overcame the problem through the love and support of his wife. If he works on the pornography case he might get addicted again.

4. Dropping in something completely out of our character's control. So, character follows the bad guy in his spare time, stows away on the bad guy's plane, his wife tied up just feet from him, and the plane crashes, stranding the three of them in the mountains, and he finds out the bad guy is his wife's half-brother, and out of love for his wife, wants to save the half-brother's life.

I know, a convoluted story, but as an example, we have all the necessary elements for tension: a love interest, a career goal, a time bomb, a wounded hero, and a dangerous setting.

Takeaway: Tension keeps a reader turning pages well into the night. Conflict makes a reader toss the book aside if it's overdone.

Exercises:

1. Go through the first five pages of a favorite book and highlight the tension in those pages.
2. Notice where the tension is in the dialog, where it's in the internal thoughts of the character, and where it's in the narrative or description.
3. Go through your work in progress and do the same. Revise as needed.

Romantic Tension

Sounds like an oxymoron, doesn't it? After all, who wants romance and tension at the same time? You do. I do. And readers do, too.

Romance draws your male and female protagonists together with promises of a happy ending inherent. Tension is what keeps them apart throughout the story, raises questions about whether they should be together, causes them to assess their goals and priorities, offers an opportunity for the antagonist to have a say in the matter, and keeps the story moving forward.

Face it, if boy meets girl, boy gets girl in the first chapter, the romance is pretty much tied in a knot for the rest of the story.

So how do we create the tension in a romance without having the characters constantly fighting, breaking up, and making up? One or two rounds of that in a story is more than enough.

Each character needs to have a back story. Not only about where he went to college or what kind of car she drives. This romantic back story should include past relationships, the lie the character believes about themselves, their dreams or goals regarding their romantic future, and the obstacles that keeps them from achieving their romantic goal. Think of romance as the ribbon that ties the characters together, and their back story as the scissors threatening to cut that ribbon. Over and over again.

For example, Bob had a girlfriend in college who dumped him for a rich frat guy. The lie he believes is that no girl could possibly love him for himself; he needs to make lots of money and be successful. The problem is that the more he works and the more stuff he acquires, the less time he has for a girlfriend.

Sue longs to have the marriage her parents had. They fell in love in sixth grade and were together ever since. But, the guy she fell in love with in high school ended up getting her pregnant and then leaving her before the baby was born. The lie she believes is that there are no happily-ever-afters, and no man is going to want her. She's damaged goods. So she holds all men at arm's length.

In your story, you could have Bob meet Sue at work. He's attracted to her but manages to work through every date he makes with her, which confirms her belief that no man should be depended on. Sue doesn't tell Bob about her daughter, so she has to work hard to keep that secret, and when Bob finds out, he believes she's just like every other woman--out to take what she can get. After all, she probably tried to trick some poor guy into marrying her by getting pregnant.

Bob's beliefs and Sue's are at odds with each other. If they both stick to their guns, they won't get together.

Work them through their problems, get them to change their belief system, and get them together by the end of the book, or at least to a point where the reader understands there's a very good chance they will get together.

Takeaway: Readers want to see a reason why the boy and girl can't get together, then see them change enough so they will.

Exercises:

1. Look at your current work in progress. Is there any romance in it? If not, why not? If so, how can you up the stakes so they don't get together until at least past the halfway point of the book?
2. Pick five pages at random from your work in progress. Print them out. Highlight the romantic tension on the page in one color. Highlight the romance in another color. Tension should outweigh romance.
3. If the thought of writing a romance makes your eyes cross, watch a good movie such as Sleepless in Seattle, Ghost, Kate and Leopold, or Leap Year.

Antagonist and Instigator

When I was a kid, my mom had two nicknames for me: antagonist and instigator. She called me the first when I insisted on playing every game by the rules and got angry with the other kids who didn't want to play that way. She called me the second when things were going too smoothly and too quietly and so I would push my sister or take my brother's toy, just to get a reaction.

Little did I know I was already in training to be a writer.

Every good story needs the hero and the heroine, maybe a little romance to keep them coming back to each other, and a little conflict to keep the story going until its satisfying conclusion.

But your story needs more than that. Your story needs an antagonist and an instigator.

The antagonist is the character who tries to keep your hero/heroine from getting what they want. The antagonist isn't always an evil villain, although he could be. Your antagonist's goals should be the opposite of what your hero/heroine wants. For example, if your hero wants to get elected as dog catcher in his town, the antagonist might be the other person running in the election. Who might also be the hero's wife/love interest. They both think they will be the best dog catcher this town ever had. And they might have completely opposing views of how to accomplish that goal.

The instigator, on the other hand, could be a completely different character. This is the person who appears mid-way through the book and shakes things up when the action is slowing down or the story is going along just a little too well. The instigator could be the lady from the SPCA who comes in to do a lecture on spaying and neutering, which both candidates are against. Or the instigator could be the mayor who wants to cut the position of dog catcher from the budget. Or the instigator might be the tree hugger from the hero's back story who knows that in a past life he worked with a perfume company that did experiments on animals and thinks that's why the hero now wants to be dog catcher, to provide a steady supply of animals for one of those companies.

The antagonist and the instigator could be the same person, but if they are, you must let the reader know early in the book that there is more depth to this character than simply wanting different goals. A story is more rounded if these characters are different people. No fair springing this on the reader like, "Oh, by the way, as you know I used to protest at these perfume companies and I remember seeing you clock in every day. I know why you're running for this position."

Antagonists up the ante, keep the conflict tense, and give readers a reason to keep reading your book. The instigator will provide more opportunities for your hero/heroine to prove themselves, and will introduce another subplot which readers love.

Antagonists and instigators – consider introducing both these characters into your story, and watch the tension and the action increase as all of these people try to accomplish their own personal goals.

Takeaway: It is almost impossible to have too much tension and conflict in a story.

Exercises:

1. Review your list of characters. Can one of them serve as an antagonist and one as an instigator?
2. There is no rule about having only one antagonist or one instigator. Can you up the ante by having another character play one of those roles, even if only for one specific plot line?
3. Multiple and conflicting plot lines can also serve as antagonists or instigators. Non-human characters such as animals, weather, and the elements can also add depth to the plot.

Recycling for Writers

We hear so much lately about carbon footprints, greenhouse effect, reduce, reuse, and recycle, that I have kind of closed my ears to all the talk. For me, most of the chatter seems intent on bringing on panic and inducing us to buy into the latest gimmick. In most cases, "they" have an agenda all their own.

But that's not what this post is about. Today I want to share an idea about how writers can recycle. And no, I'm not talking about printing on the back side of paper, although that is one thing you could do. I don't mean about refilling print cartridges and laser cartridges, although that is a good way to save money. And I'm not even going to suggest you walk to the library or the post office, even though walking is a great form of exercise and saves money on gas.

No, I'm going to talk to you about recycling ideas.

If you're anything like me, sometimes ideas for books come at the same speed as breathing. I have folders with outlines penciled on the back of a restaurant napkin because I overheard a conversation from the next table. I have notebooks filled with scrawlings about the people I watched at an airport that I was certain would make a great book. I have pictures pulled from magazines, articles from newspapers, and brochures from visitor centers that I was certain would make a good story.

And I think I was right. But that's not the kind of recycling ideas I mean.

The kind I mean is the book you wrote last week, last year, last decade, maybe even last century, that has languished in a drawer or on a hard drive because, although the story was there, something was missing. Maybe you tried writing from a different point of view. A different genre. A different world. And although you pushed on, forged ahead, and pressed toward the goal, the story fell flat in some indefinable way.

Here's what I suggest:

Take the story and divide it into three books. Turn it into a family saga, a generational epic, or maybe just a series with the same main characters working their way through their character arc. Maybe what's wrong with the original story is that it was really too big for the story you tried to fit it into. Kind of like trying to wedge yourself into your high school gym shorts. Too much content and not enough material. Add some more material in the form of plot layers, the ones you would have put in originally except you had to keep word count in mind. Create some new characters, the ones you would have included but didn't want to confuse the reader with too many new faces. If the original was a romance, add some suspense. If it was a western, add some romance. If it was a speculative, start it in the past. If it was a sci-fi, start it on earth.

The key is, try something completely different. And if the thought of writing a family epic, a generational saga, or a series scares you to death, do it anyway. The worst that can happen is you won't write the books and the original will continue to languish. In the meantime, you will have learned some important things about yourself as a writer.

And how would I know this, you might ask? Because I have done this very thing to a story I wrote that I loved in its original format, but that seemed flat in some way. I divided the story into three, hacked up the original premise, threw out some plot lines, added two new sets of characters, changed some names, increased the romance and the tension, and came up with the outline for a three-book generational saga.

And the exciting thing is that even though I haven't written these books yet, I am stoked about the new faces in the mix.I know when I get ready to write this series, I'll be more excited and more focused on the brand I'm trying to create for myself as a writer of historical suspense.

Sounds like a win-win-win situation to me.

Takeaway: There is no such thing as a bad story; just some stories aren't quite done yet.

Exercises:

1. Pull out an old story. Look at the characters and the plot. How could you start the story twenty years ago? Fifty? A hundred?
2. Could you tell this same story from the perspective of three different characters? Think about the movie, Point of View. Told from half a dozen POV's, with each one revealing new information and carrying the story forward a little further.
3. Maybe the story you're struggling with just needs a different voice. Write the first chapter from the point of view of a different character. Does this change the story for you?

FITTING IN THE RESEARCH

Making Research Fun

I've seen the way some authors' eyes nearly roll up into their heads at the word, "research". After all, that's just dry, boring stuff. We're always told to 'write what we know'. If we have to research a topic, we aren't writing what we know.

I used to write what I knew. My recently-published novel is about an accountant, which is what I trained for. Except everybody thinks accountants are boring. So I went looking for an exciting accountant, and I found one in a forensics accountant. No, they don't count dead bodies -- forensics accountants uncover hidden assets for estates, divorces, and the IRS.

My character, Carly Turnquist, uncovers dead bodies -- or at least, she gets involved in mysteries and murders, has her life threatened a couple of times, finds some missing money, and saves her daughter from doom. All in the first book.

The funny thing was, even while I was writing what I knew -- accounting -- there were things I didn't know. Like the details about numbered companies. How to distinguish if someone died from a plunge over a cliff or a knock on the head. How to suffocate someone by plugging up a chimney. How the banking system works in a small town.

When I started writing historical suspense, I needed to do a lot more research. So I found locations, topics, and characters that caught my attention, and wove them into a novel. My first historical suspense includes a woman running from her husband, a Pinkerton agent who works for said husband, a bank manager who embezzled from his bank, and a boarding house lady who I envision as looking like Miss Marple. The year is 1882, and the location is Indian Rocks in Florida.

How did I come up with these details? My dad was a Pinkerton agent at one time. I worked in the banking industry and had some idea how a manager could finagle a naïve woman on the run into doing his dirty work for him by cooking the books. I have a friend who had a condo in Indian Rocks and the idea of a story set there before tourism took hold caught my attention. And the boarding house lady? I love Agatha Christie's work.

Research doesn't need to be boring, dry, or dusty, if you select a topic you really enjoy. Work together different parts of stories from different regions, and see what you come up with. Take some liberties with locations and eras. Craft a character based on someone who really lived during that time, but mix up the details with other characters. And even if you're writing a contemporary story, don't be afraid to toss in a few details that you don't know all the ins and outs about. And then do some research.

Another novel I recently completed is about a woman from the present and a man from the past who meet. I've had to do some research on both characters in order to get the details straight. The Internet is my initial tool. Then I use books, newspaper archives, diaries, and museums.

Takeaway: If your story is exciting, your research should be even more exciting.

Exercises:

1. What don't you know that you'd like to know more about? Do the research and weave those details or facts into your current work in progress.
2. Read a book in a genre other than what you usually write. For example, if you prefer contemporary stories, read a historical. Like Regency-era? Read a Biblical-era fiction.
3. Devise a way to store your research materials so you can find what you need. Binders and folders work well for printed materials. Writing software such as Scrivener and One-Note offer opportunities to save digital files including web pages.

Research Trips

Since I started writing historical fiction, I have undertaken quite a few research trips. Truth be told, I hesitated to write historical because I thought I didn't know enough history to write credibly. And I was correct. So, aside from taking university courses in history, how was I going to get the information I needed?

Answer: Research trips.

I hear you already: I don't have the money, the time.

You do, because a lot of the work of your research trips starts right at home. A research trip can be an afternoon, a day, an overnight, or however long you want or need it to be. The cool thing about research is it opens new plot elements, new location ideas, and even births new ideas for other books.

There are many ways to do a research trip, but this is my method:

1. Internet – do whatever research you can on the Internet. Search for the location of your book, and you are bound to find numerous websites with good information. If the location is real, most towns and cities have a Chamber of Commerce, many have a Historical Society or museums. Find out what happened in that town in the past and look for specialty museums such as mining, farming, flight, cars, and industrial. I print out whatever I find AND save the pages as HTML in case my editor wants to know where I got this information. Use trusted sources as much as possible.
2. If your town is fictional, look for towns in the area of your setting. Glean one interesting fact from several different towns, tweak it a little, and use it in your book as the thing that makes the town different. For example, if your town is set in the Nappa Valley in California, maybe it could be the town where the factory that prints wine bottle labels is located. Maybe the town didn't repeal prohibition until ten years after the rest of the state. And maybe wine is only served on Sundays in restaurants in the town.

3. Library – your local library is a treasure house of information without leaving home. Many libraries offer websites where you can request books from other library branches in the system and you can pick them up at your local branch. Librarians are a wealth of information as well, and larger library systems will have local non-circulating sections where you can find books, maps, journals, and newspapers.

4. Go there – if you decide the only way to get the best information is to actually visit the location, do some preparation beforehand. With the information gleaned from the steps listed above, decide what is important to your story and the scenes you plan to write. I have found these are the best ways to get a feel for your location:

(a) Museums are great, but choose the ones pertinent to your story. For example, one hour in a gun museum could do more for your Civil War scene than an entire day in the history museum. I visited a heritage center/living museum in Florida and got the feeling for how humid it can be there. I recorded the sound of the cicadas, smelled the trees and damp earth, and saw how the log cabin in my book would have looked.

(b) Choose specialty museums if you have specific questions you want answers for. A recent visit to a prison museum answered the question I had about the period of time from conviction to execution in Colorado in the 1920's that I needed for a book I'm working on.A trip to a citrus museum answered questions about the citrus industry in Florida, and I learned that cattle is also a huge part of the economy there.

(c) If the location has been preserved so as to be historically accurate, go there. I went to a Pony Express station in northern Kansas to get a feel for the terrain and what the riders would have seen as they came across the prairie in 1860.

(d) Limit your location visits to two per day. If you have more than that, plan an overnight stay or two because otherwise everything you learn will all jumble together and you'll be too exhausted to absorb it all.

(e) Carry a small tape recorder with you to record your thoughts, the sounds, notes on stuff you see. Before you record somebody, tell them you're doing it, and why, and ask if it's okay. I've never been refused. When you get home, type up your notes and keep them in a file for future reference.

(f) Bring a camera with lots of extra batteries. If you're taking pictures inside a museum or display, ask about their picture-taking policy.

(g) Be ready to ask questions. Curators and volunteers love to know you're going to write about their museum. They love to share what they know about your topic. Make sure you get a business card or their name and contact information. You'll want to remember these people when your book is published. You may have other questions you need to ask later on. I met the past president of the Colorado Pony Express Association, and spent a delightful hour with him as he shared stories and information. At another location on the same trip, I met the local expert on the Pony Express who knew just about everything there was to know about the Pony Express through Nebraska.

(h) If you have time and energy left over at the end of your day, be open to visiting another site you hadn't thought about. We were in Kansas on a research trip, and we stopped in at the last remaining limestone barn in Kansas that's on its original site, just because it was there. We met some wonderful ladies who were quilting, and in the process, I got an idea for an element in my book that I hadn't thought of before – a quilt – and we met the best friend of my husband's mother. Small world.

(i) Take video in addition to pictures. Video will give a better idea of the scale of objects and how they operate. If you have a YouTube channel (and you should) ask the manager or curator or whoever is in charge if you can upload the video to your channel. I have a YouTube channel specifically for historic video, which is informative, fun, and connects my name with history.

Don't let history scare you. History is the friend of the novelist. Get out there, discover a great big world, and then write your story. Don't expect to put everything you've learned into this next book you're working on. Do expect to weave in sensory details, tidbits of information about the culture, the attitudes, the way things were. Readers love to learn as they read, as long as they don't really realize they're learning. Your book is historical, not history. But it should still be accurate as to what COULD have happened, just like the rest of your story is accurate as to this story COULD have happened just the way it's written.

Takeaway: History is our friend.

Exercises:

1. Start locally--find a museum you haven't gone to and schedule in a day trip.

2. Spread your wings--where are you going on your next trip/vacation/long weekend? Find a museum to visit. I use Wikipedia, search for "list of museums in (state)" sort it by city or region, and see what the area has to offer.

3. Look up museums on the Internet that you're interested in, then plan a trip around that museum. For instance, I wanted to go to a museum about gliders to get information for a novel I was writing. I searched on Glider Museums, found the Silent Wings Museum in Lubbock, Texas. As it happened, we stay overnight in Amarillo when we travel to Texas, and Lubbock is nearby. So it was easy to tuck that museum into our trip.

Pocket Folders for Research Materials

We visited Texas for a research trip, where we focused on ranching and farming for a series I'm writing which, although set in Colorado, will still include many common details about cattle ranching in general, specifically non-irrigated ranching and wide open spaces. We also visited several other historic sites such as a fort and an aquarium for potential future books and for overall knowledge.

I love to ask the What If questions: What If cattle rustlers figured out a way to change the brands? What If my heroine came to work at the district court this morning and found a body in her chair? What If my hero's prize bull stampedes through my neighbor's yard and kills her prize cow?

One of the things that helped me stay organized were some pocket folders I'd purchased. Actually, they were more of a pocket than a folder -- a plastic pouch with a zipper. You could see through the plastic, even though the folders were different colors. I was able to categorize my papers for the travel details, receipts, museums we visited, people we talked to--all those bits of paper I struggle to keep tabs on in the car.

When we toured a ranch and farm museum, I put the brochures and information into a pocket I'd set up for ranch and farm research. We visited several old forts, and I used a folder to collect that information. The Dallas Aquarium provided some interesting information for another story where my heroine finds a body in -- you guessed it, an aquarium.

In the old days, I would have printed out my pictures and tucked them into the appropriate pocket. Now I can save the pictures on a CD and include them in the pocket. All of my research in one handy place, in a plastic folder I can see through. I can move the information to other folders if at some point I focus my research more succinctly, or if I combine several story ideas into one.

Getting more organized helps me be more productive, more concise in my writing, and helps the story have those details that help the reader experience the setting. Whether you write historical or contemporary or futuristic, research abounds that's just waiting to be gathered, categorized, and used in our stories.

Takeaway: Getting organized takes an investment of time, but in the long run, will save time.

Exercises:

1. Purchase some zippered folders and label them. I bought mine at a discount store, Big Lots, but office supply stores or stores that sell office supplies might also carry them.
2. Decide how you want your materials categorized--by book, by topic, by era. It's your system--you choose.
3. Once you have your system, add materials as you acquire them, then use them.

Nuggets of Ideas

On a research trip to California, we stayed in a bed-and-breakfast situation, sharing meals with our host family. They were a delightful couple, and during one of our conversations, she mentioned she'd been working on a short story for a number of years. I asked some questions, and finally she admitted it was more a novella, because it was too long for a short story. When I suggested perhaps it was truly a novel, which was why she was struggling to finish it, she said she didn't think she could never write a full-length novel.

When I confided that I write novels, she wanted to know where I got my ideas. I told her my ideas come to me because I'm always looking for another idea for another book.

So I shared with her – as I'm sharing with you now – where I get my ideas. Try out a few. We have about a month left in the summer, and the weather is perfect for getting out and about.

So where do I look for ideas?

Everywhere.

On this trip, we visited Echo Canyon, the setting for a Pony Express novel I've written, as well as a historical fiction I penned. The palisades, box canyons, and caves in the walls of the canyon provide good fodder-and settings-for a couple of scenes in each book, and for more scenes in the next book I plan to write about the Pony Express. It's a timeless topic that people love to read about.

We went to an aviation museum. While there, we learned about a PBY, kind of a flying boat, that was used to hunt down and destroy submarines. If you have watched Raiders of the Lost Ark, that same plane is in one of the scenes. I got to thinking about a pilot who is sent to hunt down a submarine but mistakenly fires on a small ship, sinking it and sending survivors into the water. He can't admit he made a mistake, but that memory haunts him for years, and how he decides to make restitution to the families without telling them who he is. Or maybe he designs the PBY so he could land on the water to rescue shipwrecked sailors.

We went to a firearms museum set on the grounds of the Winchester House, which gave me ideas about what if the house was a B&B, and a body was found in the formal garden one morning.

We went on a tour of the USS Hornet, a World War 2 aircraft carrier. There were so many nooks and crannies – plenty of places to hide a body.

On the way home, we stopped at Cove Fort, originally built as a way station in 1867, which gave me lots of fodder and research material for another historical suspense set at a similar fort in a similar time period.

So you see, ideas are everywhere you look. The trick is to let the ideas flow, look at the setting in a different time period or from a different perspective, and allow the characters to speak to you.

Takeaway: When you are attuned to your surroundings, finding ideas won't be a problem; making the time to write all the books will be your struggle.

Exercises:

1. Where was the last unusual setting you visited? Come up with a one-line description for a book set there.
2. Keep a notebook, a journal, a list on your phone or computer, of the ideas you generate during your travels.
3. No travel planned? Make a point to schedule in a visit to a local museum, historic location, tourist attraction, or park, and allow your creative muse to surface.

Historical Markers

There we were, hurtling down the road at about seventy-five miles an hour at ten o'clock at night, when I uttered those words my husband has come to dread: "Oh, look, a historical marker one mile ahead on the right."

He sighed and nodded. We paced off the mile and watched for the next sign. He slowed the car and pulled off the highway. I focused my camera in the general direction of where I thought the marker stood, and finally located the sign. Click! went the camera, and we were off again, racing down the road in the pitch darkness. As we traveled along, I retrieved the photo and read what text. In this case, it was the story of a small town in Texas that lasted only about five years because the townspeople couldn't get title to their land.

Hmmm – might make an interesting plot for a book.

Wait, there was another sign. And then another. That night we stopped a number of times, snapping pictures and moving on. I decided this had to be the most unique method of research I'd come up with. Simply taking the picture and reading it later meant we could cover a lot of ground in a short period. Unlike the historical marker we'd seen in Wyoming where I'd gotten out and spent at least fifteen minutes photographing an old cemetery in the middle of nowhere. Or the time I'd simply stood at the base of a mountain in Utah and looked around me at the surrounding countryside, trying to imagine the wagon trains passing by, perhaps camping at this very spot in Echo.

Historical markers serve an important purpose in our research. They can provide interesting plot ideas. They cause us to pause in our travels and consider the reason for the marker. Sometimes I stop for longer periods of time and listen to the sounds of the birds and insects, as I did at the Pony Express Station in Hanover, Kansas. I imagined the intrepid riders racing across the rolling landscape, the prairie grass tickling their horse's tummy, the birds taking wing if they rode too close.

Historical markers also remind us that not all research is done in a museum, and not all information can be found in books. Sometimes we just need to get out on those open highways, those side roads, and see what's there.

Historical markers take us close to the location, the land, the surroundings of a particular point in time. This nearness can give us a better understanding of what happened.

Historical markers also provide credibility to some interesting events that might be difficult to locate in a history book. Many of these events are regional or even specific to this one single spot on the earth, and might not be written about in other books.

This country has a lot of history, and regardless of your genre, you can always find fodder for your next novel. Even if you don't write historical, imagine using the plot line that someone comes up with a deed to New York City where the land was deeded not to Dutch settlers but to a British explorer who left all his earthly goods to the Queen of England. Similar to the marker for the ghost town in Texas with a modern-day twist. What would be the implications of such a deed?

Takeaway: Historical markers remind us that everyone's story is important.

Exercises:

1. Many states have a historical markers database or listing you can access online. Look for some in your area and visit them.
2. If you can't go to the location, you can still read about them online. Store the information away. Jot down notes.
3. Choose three historical markers from different states at random, then come up with a one-line sentence describing a book you could write using that information.

Not Just the Facts, Ma'am (or Sir)

Not so very long ago, I didn't think I could write historical fiction. My excuse? I didn't know enough 'history' to write a story set in bygone times.

Then I saw a photo in the newspaper of the police officer who accompanied Lee Harvey Oswald from the courtroom when Jack Ruby shot him.

And I was hooked.

As part of my research, I read many books about that time period (early 60's) and decided the civil rights movement wasn't what I wanted to write about. My story would be about a police officer who is assigned to investigate the shooting of a presidential candidate (not the president), and the lady journalist who is assigned to write a series of stories about the assassination.

In doing my research, I realized there was only one instance in the 1950's where both parties nominated new candidates. In other words, no incumbent. And that was exactly what I needed.

Hence my book, Counterfeit Honor, set in – where else? Denver, 1956. I could visit the site of the fictional murder--the Brown Palace. I went to the original police station, now a performing arts building. I strolled through alleyways in the downtown area, and I went to the confluence area where several scenes take place.

You, too, can write historical fiction. Here are the steps I took to writing this first book, and it's the same process I've used to write a book set in 1882 Florida, when I'd never even been to Florida until I was almost done writing this book. And it's the same process for my 1860 Pony Express novel, my 1858 Oregon Trail novel, and my 1948 Colorado ranch story.

1. Come up with an idea. Don't worry about the time period right now. Just come up with the story, the plot, the characters. In Counterfeit Honor, the photo in the newspaper sparked the story. In my Pony Express novel, My Surrendered Heart, the location came from visiting Echo Canyon. This location also

sparked the idea for my Oregon Trail novel, <u>Christmas Under the Stars.</u>

2. Decide on the time period by making the setting and time period characters in the story. Ask where these characters and setting fit best. Is this a story of lost love found? Maybe World War II. Is this a story of going beyond what is comfortable? Perhaps the setting should be 1850's America during the Westward Expansion. A story about faith that divides is well-set during the Civil War.

3. Narrow down the time frame by doing some research on what else was going on in the area and the world during these years. For example, if traveling by stagecoach instead of train is integral to the plot, set the book before the Transcontinental train is completed. In my Florida Detective series book, <u>Subterfuge</u>, I needed a character to travel by stagecoach, so I had to set it before 1885 when the train came to southern Florida.

4. Then read everything you can lay your hands on set in that time period. I like to get books from the children's library, since they contain the most important facts. I search out diaries, newspaper accounts, archives, anything written in the time period.

5. Watch movies set in that time. If your book is set in the 1900's, watch movies made in that time period.

6. When at all possible, visit the place where your book is set. Online research, reading, and movies are all great sources of information, but there is nothing like standing on the actual site. For example, I'd heard that in Florida the air is so humid you feel as if you're drinking each breath. I didn't understand that until I stood in the middle of a swamp in Florida, listening to the insects and birds, drinking the air.

One of my most memorable research trips was to follow the Pony Express route in Kansas and Nebraska. I stood where the riders had raced across the prairie a hundred and fifty years ago. I stood in the wagon ruts going through Scotts Bluff. At times, I could have sworn I heard the pounding hooves, the creaking saddle leather, the crack of the whips on the backs of the oxen pulling the wagons.

Be brave enough to take that story that's been floating around in your mind, that you've kept submerged for years, perhaps, because the setting was in a time period you felt you knew nothing about, and write down your idea. Make the time period and setting as important as the characters and plot. Then research. Immerse yourself in what is going on in YOUR story, YOUR setting, YOUR time period.

Takeaway: You don't have to learn everything about a time period. Learn just enough to write your book.

Exercises:

1. Go to the library today and check out some books, especially from the children's section, on the time period you're interested in.
2. Go online and do some more research.
3. Plan a research trip to visit the location you're writing about. The details you absorb will show in your writing.

ODDS & SODS (I.E. OTHER STUFF)

Ghostwriting isn't Spooky Business

Ghostwriting, or writing for somebody else where it will appear as if THEY wrote the article or book, isn't something new. You can go back to the Bible and find instances where the Apostle Paul had someone else write his letters for him. He dictated, they wrote. Several books of the Old Testament were penned by scribes as the "real author" dictated.

Ghostwriting is much the same.

The Author, whose name will be on the cover, usually has an idea of what they want, some notes and research, a story, maybe an outline, some chapters written, a defined market for the book, and maybe even a publisher.

The Writer (that's you), brings a combination of experience, ability, excitement about the project, the time and energy to complete the writing, some ideas about how to finish, and, in some cases, advice on how to format, publish, and market the writing.

In essence, you are selling your work to someone else to use as their own.

Wait a minute. That's plagiarism, isn't it? No. Because you are selling the work to them. It's like a (gulp) job. If you worked for a company that builds houses, their name is on the house, not yours, because they paid you to do it.

Doesn't ghostwriting steal your creativity? I would hasten to say no; it feeds creativity because it provides an outlet, it provides the opportunity to learn as we work, and it provides the resources necessary to fund our own personal projects.

Some writers say they don't want anything published that doesn't have their name on it. The Apostle Paul, who wrote two-thirds of the New Testament, doesn't have one book named after him. Be honest: seeing your name on the cover of a book fills your heart with pride. Are we writing for the glory of God, or for our own pride? If we're writing for God's glory, then it won't matter whose name is on the cover.

Ghostwriting is a great way to generate income when you're between projects. You can hone your writing skills, particularly if you're asked to complete a project that is outside what you usually write. The process can develop strong friendships with the Author as you work together, often hearing intimate details about someone else's life. It's a good way to put you in your right place: as transcriber of God's stories.

Ghostwriting projects abound. You can find them through groups and organizations such as The Christian Pen, through online writing groups, publishers, and through personal referrals. Let folks know you're open to ghostwriting, keep improving your writing skills, and allow God to drop that perfect project into your lap.

Always have a contract that spells out the details and contingencies of your agreement. Expect to spend some time talking with the Author, and build in time for research. Follow through and complete the assignment ahead of time as much as is it in your power to do. If you would like a sample contract, click on the Ghostwriting tab on my blog at www.HiStoryThruTheAges.wordpress.com.

Takeaway: Ghostwriting is simply another way to get your work out there without getting your name out there.

Exercises:

1. Make a list of the skills you could offer another writer. Think about those skills you use right now that you're not getting paid for. For example, do you judge contests? Are you a member of a critique group? Do you help others brainstorm ideas? All of these are skills used in ghostwriting.
2. Do some research online into how much many companies charge for a ghostwriter.
3. Add a page to your website outlining your skills, prepare a contract, and tell others that you are interested in ghostwriting assignments.

Interview Your Characters

"Getting to know you, getting to know all about you. . . "

When I sit down to create characters for a new project, this tune runs through my head. This is one truth writers ought to embrace: we need to know our characters better than anybody in our book does. Better than our readers will know them by the time they finish reading.

If we don't know our characters, we'll tend to write flat, one-dimensional people, like paper dolls who are simply wearing an outfit called "their story", and are as interchangeable as--well, a paper doll.

Another danger in not knowing our characters is we'll write three chapters getting to know them, wasting paper and the reader's time as we plow our way through their back story, their history, until we finally get to the point where our story really starts, about halfway through Chapter 4.

There are many methods to get to know your characters. Some of these require you to sit down and fill out a questionnaire that would cause most of us to lose our minds or at the very least, our excitement about our stories. While the details and minutiae of these questionnaires might work for some, many of us will struggle to answer what our character's third grade teacher said that made him decide to become a private investigator twenty years later.

Bored with filling out forms, making up answers to questions I hadn't even thought of, and wanting to get on with the process of writing, I came up with a faster and more direct way to get to know my characters--I interview them.

I pretend I'm a famous talk show host and my character is a guest on my show. As a famous talk show host, I know everybody in the world will want to hear what I have to say and how I can make my character squirm on live TV. So I come up with questions that will cause said squirming because I know how the story goes and what secrets my character is trying to keep.

Go ahead. Be catty. Be devious. Dig up the dirt. What would someone who reads one of those supermarket tabloids want to know about your character? And why would your character not want to tell the truth, not want to break a confidence, not want you to know everything about them? Because characters are real people, and real people rarely tell the whole truth and nothing but the truth.

Even good people hide some things, hold back some things, try to make themselves look good perhaps at the expense of another.

Here is a list of questions I typically ask to get started:

1. How did you get the job you have?
2. What's your background that qualified you for that job?
3. Tell me about ___________ (the inciting incident in the book).
4. Tell me about ___________ (could be the love interest, the villain, the hero/heroine. Whoever is making this character's life difficult or messy in some way)
5. Tell me about ____________ (whatever you know your character doesn't want to talk about. A past hurt, a secret, a rumor, an innuendo – anything that will make it look like this character isn't telling all)
6. Bring up a topic that's in the news now, and tie it into this character and the plot in some way. For example, if the character is a forest ranger, and poaching by forest rangers is in the news, ask what he thinks should be done to poachers and then what should be done to poachers who are also guardians of the woodland. Watch him squirm.
7. Ask what the character sees in his/her future.

By the time you ask and your character answers these questions, you should have a good idea of what motivates your character, what scares your character, what your character is trying to hide and why, the lie your character believes, what the internal and external conflicts are, and the growth arc of your character.

In the next chapter, you will find two sample interviews I've done for my main characters in <u>Counterfeit Honor.</u>

Takeaway: Finding out your character's deepest secret so you can blab it across the pages of your book is a good thing.

Exercises:

1. Choose one character from your current work in progress and interview him/her.
2. What questions didn't he/she want to answer? Why? Add this to your back story for this character.
3. How can another character capitalize on knowing this information? Does this change your story in some way? Write in that new plot line.

Sample Interviews

Interview of Margaret Buchanan, journalist with the Rocky Mountain News of Denver, who was on the spot as an eyewitness to the murder of both Thomas Waterman and Arthur Crawford by Sally Smithers of Book Reviews R Us.

SS: Hello, Margaret. Thank you for taking time to talk with us today.

MB: My pleasure, Sally.

SS: Your face has been on the front page of the News for several days now.

MB: Yes, and before that, I was buried in Section D under the Lifestyle column.

SS: Still, not a bad start to a journalism career. First job, right out of college, and you get on with the News.

MB: I agree it may seem like a good start, but obituaries and engagement parties isn't the kind of writing I want to do. I want to make a difference with my writing.

SS: Don't you think handling a loved one's death in a compassionate way is important?

MB: That's true, but it isn't my life plan.

SS: So how did you land this job with the News?

MB: Truth be told, I wanted to prove to my parents that I could make it on my own in the very male oriented world of journalism. The News is the only paper that offered me a job.

SS: So tell us a little about your background.

MB: I was born and raised in Georgia, the daughter of southern gentility. My parents expected little else of me than to marry well and give them lots of grandchildren. I had other ideas.

SS: Such as?

MB: To have an adventure, to see more of the country than just Georgia peach groves, and to prove that women can do more than just become teachers or nurses or secretaries. After all, this is 1956, not 1856.

SS: Tell us about the murder.

MB: Which one?

SS: That's right. You were right there to witness two murders. Were you afraid?
MB: Honestly, it happened so quickly I didn't have time to be afraid. At least, not until later. Then my knees shook when I realized just how close I'd been to not just one killer, but two.
SS: Tell us about your policeman.
MB: First of all, he's not my policeman. He's very much his own man.
SS: What was your first impression of Trevor McGonigle?
MB: The first time I saw him, I knew instantly that my heart was in trouble. As was my story.
SS: Did you work well together on the case?
MB: We certainly did, so long as I didn't write about it, didn't investigate it, and gave him all the information I had.
SS: Doesn't sound like you were getting a fair opportunity to put your best foot forward.
MB: That's true. And then I also had to deal with a district attorney dogging my steps, a blackmailer with a huge grudge, and an editor who was being pressured to drop the series of stories.
SS: But it all worked out in the end, didn't it?
MB: Yes, Sally, it all worked out.
SS: Well, Margaret, it sounds like you're not going to give away any secrets.
MB: No, Sally, I'm not. If you want to know the ending, you'll just have to read my articles.
SS: Thank you, Margaret. And dear readers, join us next week for an interview with Trevor McGonigle, the Denver Police officer who, along with Margaret, wrapped this case up in record time.

Interview of Trevor McGonigle, detective with the Denver Police Department, who is in charge of the Waterman and Crawford murder investigations, by Sally Smithers of Book Reviews R Us.
SS: Hello, Detective. Or can I call you Trevor?
TM: Trevor is fine, Sally. Oops -- sorry, I spilled my coffee. I guess I'm a little nervous.

SS: A big hulking man like you with a gun tucked into an underarm holster isn't nervous of me, is he?
TM: Not of you, no. Just that this is my first interview.
SS: Understandable. Now, Trevor, tell us a little about yourself.
TM: Not much to tell. I was born in Denver, joined the Army after high school. I fought in the Korean War. After I came home, I joined the police force.
SS: You won a medal in the war, didn't you? Tell us about that.
TM: I'd rather not talk about it.
SS: Oh, Trevor, our readers would love to hear about a war hero.
TM: I said, I'd rather not talk about it.
SS: Oh, those dark smoldering eyes are throwing daggers at me. I guess that topic is off limits. Tell us about being a policeman in Denver.
TM: I love my job.
SS: Didn't we hear about some trouble with the mob?
TM: Nothing except they don't like us and we don't like them.
SS: Oh, Trevor, I think you're being coy with me. Weren't you instrumental in a big bust just a few weeks ago?
TM: Can't talk about that. Next question.
SS: Oh, I love mysterious men. Okay, tell us about the Waterman murder.
TM: Thomas Waterman, the Democratic Party's candidate for president, was killed at the Brown Palace. Your readers already know that, Sally.
SS: Yes, but they want the story behind the story. He was shot by a crazy man from out east, wasn't he?
TM: We might not completely understand Arthur Crawford's motivations, but I don't think it's fair to classify him as crazy.
SS: What drives a man to commit such an atrocious act?
TM: Desperation. I think he thought he'd done all he could by other means.
SS: So who killed Crawford?
TM: Could we talk about some of the programs the police department is involved in?

SS: A subtle segue into a new topic. You're learning fast. Okay, I'll bite. What are some of the other programs the police department is involved in?
TM: Well, we've been studying some of the larger departments around the country, such as New York City and Los Angeles. And we're very close to implementing a narcotics squad, an internal affairs division, and community resource officers.
SS: What about women in the Denver Police?
TM: In the past, police matrons were relegated to being file clerks and evidence clerks. We are developing a program to integrate our female police officers into the regular ranks. Give them the same chance at promotion that the men have.
SS: Interesting. Tell us about Margaret Buchanan.
TM: You probably know as much about her as I do.
SS: I doubt that, Trevor. You've been seen around town socially.
TM: I'm sure a woman as intelligent and beautiful as Marg -- Miss Buchanan is seen around town often.
SS: Perhaps, but she seems to prefer your company.
TM: Now, what would a woman like Miss Buchanan see in a lowly police detective?
SS: Good question. Tell me, what are your plans for the future?
TM: Do a good job. Maybe eventually be Denver's first Irish American police chief.
SS: Well, there you have it, readers. A man who is definitely going places. Margaret Buchanan, watch your step. You might just have some competition!

Split Personality?

We have a confession to make. Leeann is my alter ego. And she and I talk. We were chatting the other day. She wanted to know why I created her.

"I was writing and hoping to publish in two different genres: historical suspense and contemporary suspense. I didn't want to confuse my readers by writing in different genres."

"How did you pick my name?"

"My husband's middle name is Lee, his mother's middle name is Ann, and my mother's nickname in nursing school was Betts."

"Isn't making up a name illegal?"

"Not unless I'm trying to avoid a legal claim or defraud somebody."

She chewed on her bottom lip, a funny habit she has. "How do you keep us straight?"

I smiled at her. "First of all, you're cute and perky and all the things I'm not. Second, you write different stories than I write."

"Such as?"

"Most of my historical suspense are stories about women who have made some bad choices, and now they want to straighten out their lives. Your stories are about stronger, quirkier women who are driven to excel."

"Sounds like you."

Now it was my turn to chew my bottom lip. Maybe she inherited that trait from me. "But the women you write about don't know they are strong. Or quirky. And the women I write about are just like me. Hoping it's true that God is a God of second chances. And finding out He is."

"So we're different but the same?"

I patted her on the head like she was an obedient puppy. "Exactly."

Takeaway: Creating an alter ego or using a pen name allows you to create a whole new persona for yourself.

Exercises:

1. Do you write in different genres?
2. Do you write in the same genre, but perhaps have different levels of violence, language, and sex?
3. Do you wish sometimes you could be someone else?
4. Are you willing to double your workload by adding another blog, Facebook, Twitter, etc?

If you answered yes to two or more of these questions, you are a prime candidate for a pen name.

Digital Publishing

Having just waded through the digital publishing jungle and experienced the joy of seeing my first books available for sale on Amazon and other online retailers, it seemed perhaps I could offer some encouragement and insight for other writers. I've had several people ask me about my experience, so maybe there are more of you out there who are interested.

I decided to go with digital publishing, a.k.a. self-publishing, for a number of reasons. In no particular order, these reasons included: I wanted to get my name in front of people; I wanted to see some return on the investment sooner rather than later; my agent agreed I probably had more books in me than any one publisher would be interested in and that some of these books might have a hard time being placed with a traditional publisher; I believe I have a message that will touch somebody and make a difference for the kingdom.

All that, and yes, I'll admit it, I would like to see my name on the cover of a book before I die.

But you'll note I didn't put that reason first.

Because the truth is, if that's the only reason you're self-publishing/digitally publishing, it's the poorest reason of all.

Following is a list of the steps I took to digitally publish my books:

1. I chose an imprint (think publishing company) name. Actually I chose about ten names, researched them to make certain there were no other publishers out there with similar-sounding names, and made sure the website was available. That eliminated about eight names, so I bought the website for the one remaining which I liked better, and registered it as a d/b/a in my state.
2. I researched ISBN numbers and selected a package. How many you buy will depend on your budget and how many books you think you'll publish. For me it made sense to buy a big package because I have a lot of books. Each book format

needs its own ISBN. So, if you start with digital, you'll need one for Amazon, and one for NOOK/Smashwords. If you go to print later, you'll need another ISBN. ISBN's will run you $6 to $125 each, depending on the package you buy.

3. I researched copyright laws and checked into the cost of copyrights. You will need to register and pay for the manuscript just once regardless of how many formats you publish in. If you make changes to the manuscript, you'll need to register and pay for another copyright. I chose to register only in the US. Copyright will cost you $35 to $55 per manuscript, depending on whether it's part of a series or not.
4. Since Amazon is the biggest online retailer and sells books in many countries, it made sense to publish through Kindle Direct Publishing. It's free, mostly, and relatively easy. There are various choices to make regarding the royalty rate, whether you want to enroll the book in Kindle Select, and so on. Amazon is good about providing enough information to make informed decisions.
5. Although I did publish a book on NOOK, I later found out Smashwords is easier to use, just as free, and sends its books to NOOK as well, so I won't waste my time doing double work in the future.
6. I created a worksheet to help me stay on track so I didn't forget anything. If you go to my website, http://www.leeannbetts.com/4.html and click on the Publishing Tracking Form, you'll find the PDF I use. I like paper, so I print these out and fill them in by hand.
7. I did some research into cover design, then determined to own my covers, so I took the photographs or used royalty-free photos, and used Photoshop to design my covers. With Amazon, they provide cover templates for free if that's easier for you.

8. Once your book is published, you will then spend time learning how to market your book, how to read reports, set up your royalty accounts with your various online retailers, and get people to buy your book and post reviews. Honest reviews. Those are gold.

I suspect there are many ways to publish, and this process simply describes the paths I took. I'd love if you would share any insights you have, including ways to save time and money without giving away your rights to someone else.

Takeaway: Digital publishing does not mean you weren't good enough to be traditionally published.

Exercises:

1. Why do you want to be published?
2. Why do you think you haven't been traditionally published?
3. Would you stop writing if you knew you were never going to be published?

If your answer to question three was "no", digital publishing might be right for you.

Conference Season Ahead

As writers, we spend many hours in solitude, pecking away at the keyboard, looking up information on the Internet, or researching at the library. Conference season gives us the chance to come out of the office and get with like-minded writers.

Depending on where you live, how much time you have available, and how much money you can invest, there are many conference choices available. Finding a conference is never the problem--choosing which one or two or three to attend is.

Here is a checklist to consider as you read conference websites, newsletters, and brochures:

1. Where is the conference being held, and have I always wanted to go there? If you can tie the travel to the conference in with your current work-in-process or perhaps the next planned novel, that is even better.
2. Is the keynote speaker someone I've always wanted to hear? If so, perhaps this conference is for you. Research author credibility, publishing history, genre, and personality if you don't recognize the keynote speaker.
3. What do I expect to learn from the workshops? Repeating the same workshops conference after conference won't be the best use of your investment. Don't automatically sign up for workshops because they fit your genre--consider sitting in on some classes that you wouldn't normally choose. At one conference, I went to a class on writing horror and discovered some really spooky traits to add to my antagonists even though I write suspense.
4. What else can I accomplish while I'm there? Perhaps there is an afternoon of workshops that you aren't particularly interested in. Use the time to visit museums or attractions that work into your novel. Plan to arrive early or stay after if you absolutely must attend every class.

5. Does the conference include sessions where I will write or do homework? If so, this is probably a good choice. Imagine: a writers conference where you actually write.

Suppose you have two conferences but can only afford to go to one. How to choose without making money the only deciding factor?

1. Mark every class at both conferences and see which one offers you the most opportunities to learn.
2. Does one conference offer their sessions on CD or DVD while the other doesn't? If so, perhaps attend the one and buy the CD's of the other.
3. Have you attended one of the conferences several times? Sure, it's nice to renew old friendships, but perhaps this is the year to step out and make new friends.
4. Are you looking for an agent or a publisher? Which conference offers your more opportunities to make that connection?

Takeaway: Attending a conference will change your perspective on your writing.

Exercises:

1. Have fun, but don't get so wrapped up in attending conferences that you don't have time to write.
2. Make it a point to talk to people you don't know.
3. Take lots of notes. You will not be able to remember everything.

RESOURCES

There are many great online resources and books available regarding writing, too numerous to mention all of them here. However, I will include a list of resources that have helped me.

Writing groups:

American Christian Fiction Writers: www.acfw.com. ACFW has local chapters in most states, and offers online critique groups, online courses, and savings when registering for their conference.

Sisters in Crime: for sisters and brothers who write suspense, mystery, thriller, police or legal procedurals -- www.SistersInCrime.org. SinC has local chapters in many state and offers a discount at conferences for members.

Romance Writers of America: www.rwa.

Research:

Wikipedia: search for "list of museums in (state)"

Your local librarian -- they love to help with research

Chamber of Commerce

Historical Society -- many towns have a historical society with docents who love to talk about the history.

Conferences:

American Christian Fiction Writers: annual conference that moves around the country -- www.acfw.com/conference

Sisters in Crime: annual conference that moves around the country, as well as regional conferences -- www.SisterInCrime.org/?page=13

Killer Nashville: annual conference in Nashville, Tennessee that features forensics, crime, psychology, and more -- www.KillerNashville.com

Colorado Christian Writers Conference: annual conference held in Estes Park, Colorado -- Colorado.WriteHisAnswer.com

More Conferences:

Philadelphia Christian Writers Conference: annual conference held in Philadelphia, PA -- Philadelphia.WriteHisAnswer.com

Mount Hermon Christian Writers Conference: annual conference held in Mt. Hermon, CA -- Writers.MountHermon.org

Shaw Guides to Writers Conferences and Workshops: a great place to see if there is a conference or workshop happening some place you're traveling to or through: writing.shawguides.com

Online learning opportunities:

www.FutureLearn.com -- offers free university-quality courses that you can do at your own pace; check out Identifying the Dead, a course on forensics that takes you through a mock crime scenario, or 100 Stories, a Word War 1 course that introduces you to 100 men and women from Australia and New Zealand and the impact of the war on their lives.

www.WritersDigest.com -- offers many courses specifically for writers; usually a cost associated with these courses

Most writers' groups offer online courses, including ACFW, which are free to members

www.ChristianPen.com -- offers courses for editors and proofreaders that usually have a nominal cost

Dear Readers: Thanks for purchasing this book. If you've enjoyed it, please leave a review online wherever you usually do that.

And, if you'd like to learn more, check out the next book in the series, "More Nuggets of Writing Gold", available here: https://www.amazon.com/More-Nuggets-Writing-Gold-2/dp/1943688451

Donna lives in Denver with husband Patrick, three housemates, and two cats who rule the roost. As a hybrid author, she writes squeaky clean historical suspense and contemporary suspense. She previously published contemporary books under her alter ego of Leeann Betts, but now authors books in her name only. She has been traditionally and indie published more than 60 times in novellas, full-length novels, devotional books, and books on the writing craft. She is a member of American Christian Fiction Writers, Writers on the Rock, Pikes Peak Writers, Christian Women Writers, Faith Hope and Love Christian Writers, and Christian Authors Network; facilitates a critique group; and teaches writing classes online and in person. Donna also ghostwrites, edits, and judges in writing contests. She is also a Writing Coach, helping authors move their book projects forward. You can check that out at her FB group: https://www.facebook.com/groups/604220861766651 She loves history and research, traveling extensively for both. In her spare time, she paints like a whirling Banshee Bob Ross-style in oil on canvas, minus the Afro. You can connect with her online at www.donnaschlachter.com

Connecting Online:

www.DonnaSchlachter.com Stay connected so you learn about new releases, preorders, and presales, as well as check out featured authors, book reviews, and a little corner of peace. Plus: Receive 2 free ebooks simply for signing up for our free newsletter!
www.DonnaSchlachter.com/blog
Facebook: www.Facebook.com/DonnaschlachterAuthor
Books: Amazon: http://amzn.to/2ci5Xqq
Bookbub: https://www.bookbub.com/authors/donna-schlachter
Goodreads:
https://www.goodreads.com/search?utf8=%E2%9C%93&query=donna+schlachter
The Purpose-Full Writer:
https://www.facebook.com/groups/604220861766651
Need a writing coach? https://www.donnaschlachter.com/the-purpose-full-writer-coaching-programs

www.ingramcontent.com/pod-product-compliance
Lightning Source LLC
Chambersburg PA
CBHW060504280326
41933CB00014B/2855

* 9 7 8 1 9 4 3 6 8 8 0 5 0 *